"Reading these pages, you will understand the meaning and experience the wisdom of the ancient Eastern tradition. With warmth and compassion, Bien draws a wonderful road map to happiness. I highly recommend this book to anyone dealing with any form of suffering, but also to whomever wants to find a pathway leading to well-being and wishes to discover the magic and the healing power of being deeply present."

—Fabrizio Didonna, Psy.D., clinical psychologist and editor of *The Clinical Handbook of Mindfulness*

"In Western psyche and psychology, the pursuit of happiness is often assumed to involve doing, taking control, striving, and acquiring. In *The Buddha's Way of Happiness*, Bien invites us to stroll a very different path, an ancient Eastern way toward inner peace and contentment. Whatever one's own religion, there is deep wisdom here to read, ponder, and practice."

—William R. Miller, Ph.D., Emeritus Distinguished Professor of Psychology and Psychiatry at the University of New Mexico

"It is a radical notion to think that happiness might be found much closer than we think, or that it is not located in the places we usually look for it. In his new book, Bien invites us to consider exactly this possibility as he draws on the teachings of the Buddha, everyday examples, and the richness of diverse faith and spiritual traditions. Bien explores an expanded perspective on human happiness rooted in ancient wisdom, yet extraordinarily relevant to our time. Whether you consider yourself a Buddhist or not, there is much of value here. I recommend you see for yourself. If you do, you just might come away feeling happier!"

—Jeffrey Brantley, MD, author of *Five Good Minutes*

"Accessible and graceful, this book unfolds with a clarity that rises from a depth of practice and extends a kind invitation to others to explore the truth of these teachings for themselves. The Buddha's insights penetrate into daily life applications with philosophical understanding, meditation practices, and stories that encourage investigation and engagement with one's moment-to-moment experience of living."

> —Florence Meleo-Meyer, MS, MA, director of Oasis Professional Training and Education and senior teacher of the stress reduction program at the University of Massachusetts Medical School

"In this wise, readable book, Bien reveals the essence of ancient Buddhist psychology—the psychology of happiness—for modern readers. Then he offers practical strategies for uncovering the happiness we already possess. Recommended for anyone who seeks freedom from suffering at the deepest level."

> —Christopher K. Germer, Ph.D., clinical instructor at Harvard Medical School and author of *The Mindful Path to Self-Compassion*

The Buddha's
Way of
Happiness

healing sorrow,
transforming
negative emotion
& finding
well-being in the
present moment

Thomas Bien, Ph.D.

New Harbinger Publications, Inc.

Publisher's Note

This publication is designed to provide accurate and authoritative information in regard to the subject matter covered. It is sold with the understanding that the publisher is not engaged in rendering psychological, financial, legal, or other professional services. If expert assistance or counseling is needed, the services of a competent professional should be sought.

Distributed in Canada by Raincoast Books

Copyright © 2010 by Thomas Bien
New Harbinger Publications, Inc.
5674 Shattuck Avenue
Oakland, CA 94609
www.newharbinger.com

FSC
Mixed Sources
Product group from well-managed
forests and other controlled sources

Cert no. SW-COC-002283
www.fsc.org
© 1996 Forest Stewardship Council

Cover design by Amy Shoup
Text design by Michele Waters-Kermes
Acquired by Catharine Sutker
Edited by Nelda Street

Library of Congress Cataloging-in-Publication Data

Bien, Thomas.
   The Buddha's Way of Happiness : Healing Sorrow, Transforming Negative
Emotion, and Finding Well-Being in the Present Moment / Thomas Bien, Ph.D. ;
Foreword by Lama Surya Das.
      pages cm
   Includes bibliographical references.
   ISBN 978-1-57224-869-4 (pbk.) -- ISBN 978-1-57224-870-0 (pdf ebook) 1.
Buddhism--Psychology. 2. Emotions--Religious aspects--Buddhism. 3. Happiness--
Religious aspects--Buddhism. I. Title.
   BQ4570.P76B53 2011
   294.3'444--dc22

                                        2010043969

Printed in the United States of America

12   11   10

10   9   8   7   6   5   4   3   2   1   First printing

For Edker Matthews and Susan Hopkins,
two of the happiest people I know.

Don't look outside yourself for happiness. Let go of the idea that you don't have it. It is available within you.

—Thich Nhat Hanh, *The Heart of the Buddha's Teaching*

Contents

Foreword: Happiness and Well-Being Is the Way

by Lama Surya Das

Spiritual awakening and enlightenment is an inside job. Thank God for Buddhist wisdom and practices, and thank God Thomas Bien has done his homework.

Recent scientific research (Seligman 1998) demonstrates that we can increase our happiness in an enduring way by understanding our positive emotions and consciously encouraging those factors that are conducive to them and discouraging those that are detrimental to them. The efficacious factors include cultivating mindfulness, empathy, compassionate action, and altruism. This happiness research, along with the tools and techniques that have emerged from it, offers far more significant benefits than mere hedonism, where we try to experience as many momentarily happy feelings as possible. The new study of happiness encompasses lessons on how we can live a long, deeply meaningful, good, and true life of authentic satisfaction and fulfillment. Is this not what we all search for in our lives?

Happiness is very popular these days, perhaps even more than ever. Although time seems scarce, today many people seem to have the leisure to worry about whether or not they are happy, whether they are in the right relationship, job, or location. Or they commonly express other concerns to the extent that my therapist friends refer to them as "the worried well." Like most people, I, too, consider happiness to be of the utmost importance, especially when it comes to my own happiness and that of my loved ones! May all be happy, peaceful, and content, as the Buddha's loving-kindness prayer expresses it.

Meanwhile, as we mature and widen our circle of caring to include more and more people and creatures of all kinds in our heart-mind-spirit's warm, empathic embrace, all the wisdom of the timeless spiritual, philosophical, psychological, and humanistic traditions come into play. For happiness is the goal of human life, as the Dalai Lama of Tibet likes to say, and wisdom, both practical and transcendental, is needed to achieve it. Knowing the world is mere information, knowledge; knowing yourself is wisdom. When I become clearer, everything becomes clearer, and all my relations are clarified and harmonized. This is the heart of Buddha's attention revolution and his path of attitude transformation and spiritual awakening.

Why do happiness and lasting satisfaction so often seem too hard to achieve, like the elusive butterfly of love? Isn't it because we are too often looking for love and satisfaction in all the wrong places? An old spiritual teaching has it that God hid herself in the last place any of us would ever look to find her—within ourselves. Buddha hides within the very immediacy of *nowness*, closer than your own breath, more intimate than your own heartbeat. Everything we seek is within. That's why contentment is the ultimate form of wealth. Yet we could say that happiness comes from within and also from without, through deeper *relatedness*.

Fulfillment can come from looking deeper within your relationships, not just within yourself.

There seem to be just a few helpful techniques for effecting real change, some ancient and some modern. Research (Seligman 1998) shows that consciously learned optimism, reciprocity, and flexibility can significantly help reset habitual happiness levels that were compromised by genetic inheritance, personal biochemistry, social conditioning, individual experience, and especially the framework in which we hold those experiences—the story we tell ourselves. When mood is positively shifted through intentional mental training—usually associated these days with mindfulness, compassion development, and concentration exercises—the brain's left neocortex, involved in positive emotion, is stimulated, activated, strengthened, and boosted. Buddhist master Shantideva, the peace master of ancient India, once said, "Happiness in this world comes from thinking less about ourselves and more about the well-being of others. Unhappiness comes from being preoccupied with the self." This is the basis of Buddhist *lojong*, or attitude transformation, a spiritually refining process of mind training and heart opening.

The Buddha said, "If you think or act with a calm and bright heart-mind, then happiness follows you always, like a shadow." He outlined five kinds of happiness, which we can achieve by discovering the causes and factors conducive to it and adopting them, while relinquishing those that are detrimental to satisfaction and well-being. These five kinds of happiness are that of sense pleasure; that derived from giving and sharing, from reciprocity; that of the bliss and inner peace arising from intensely concentrated states of meditative awareness (*samadhi*) combined with mental purity; that of fulfillment stemming from insightful wisdom and profound understanding; and that of nirvanic happiness, everlasting bliss, and deathless beatitude and oneness. Buddha also long ago distinguished between mere sensual pleasure and satisfaction, on one hand, and gratification, fulfillment, and contentment on the deeper, other hand.

Today we even have a new happiness movement, including the emergent field of positive psychology, in which mental health and many of the positive aspects of mental and psychological strengths are emphasized rather than merely pathologies and mental illnesses. Happiness and its ways and means, causes and obstacles are the subject of study, and a person's happiness quotient and so-called mood thermostat, or internal set point, are being more skillfully investigated, understood, and attended to. The king of Bhutan, the last Buddhist principality in the Himalayas, has even declared that gross national happiness is the most important thing for his kingdom and government, above and beyond gross national product. Perhaps there's a lesson in there for all of us, and we might cleave to the higher ground right here and now, where we are, rather than dream of distant snow-peaked mountain ranges.

But what is happiness, really, and how do we choose it, intentionally aspire to it, and achieve it? And once achieved, how do we maintain and enjoy it without loss or deterioration, especially in these turbulent and troubled times? Is happiness simply mere pleasure: a moment on the lips, a lifetime stuck on your hips, like a fattening sweet dessert? Is there no gradation between fleeting sensual pleasure and gratification, happy feelings, good moods, deeper satisfaction, fulfillment, joyous bliss, inner peace, contentment, and heavenly nirvanic bliss? And how can we get a piece of this wondrous happiness product and joy-path action? These were some of the questions I had when I first opened Thomas Bien's remarkable, well-researched, and thoughtful book in which he eloquently addresses these pertinent and provocative issues.

It is said there are four core doctrines found in all classic happiness theories from wisdom literature, philosophy, psychology, spirituality, and self-help. Following any of them is challenging, to say the least. They are:

- Know yourself.

- Control your desires.

- Take care of what's yours.

- Remember death and mortality.

Some posit that happiness comes from being totally engaged and lost in whatever you happen to be doing at the moment. This modern notion of flow, championed by psychologist Mihaly Csikszentmihalyi, is fine, as far as it goes, and akin to the Zen Buddhist teaching of no self and no mind. However, it leaves out certain ethical, social, and health implications that might impinge on the happiness and well-being of individuals and groups in the long run, if they are entirely and consistently overlooked. Regularly indulging in the oblivion of being totally and completely lost in one of the addictive forms of unhealthy intoxication, for example, reminds us that the middle way of moderation, balance, and appropriateness is the golden rule of Buddhism: not too tight and not too loose, neither too materialistic and indulgent nor too ascetic or unworldly. Here is the secret to health, happiness, contentment, and well-being.

This is precisely where Thomas Bien comes in, with his humanistic, empirical, and nondogmatic new contribution to the emerging field of what I call positive Buddhism, showing us how the insights of the enlightened teacher of India known as the Buddha can help make us happy, healed, and whole again, by bringing us back in touch with the Garden of Eden, which is our true home and innate nature, outside time and circumstances, beyond aging and death. Bien provides us with practices and background understanding about how to cultivate, practice, develop, and actually live the Buddhist saying "There is no way to happiness; happiness is the way"—positive Buddhism emphasizing the good news that joy and the inherent freedom of being are our birthright and potential, rather than entirely dealing with suffering and its causes, the not self, and other such challenging facts of life from Buddha's ancient (yet timeless) perspective, traditionally posed in negativistic terms to exhort and motivate the old-world faithful. For we are not usually as aware of our joys and blessings—count your blessings, as they say—as we are of the least hurt, slight, or complaint. Let's strive to work on our strength and passion rather than overly focus on our weaknesses, problems, and hang-ups. Life is precious; handle with prayer.

It is not what happens to us but what we make of it that makes all the difference. Choice, intention, and motivation are pivotal and potent change agents that lie at the root of our life journey, both now and later. This is how we generate and create—consciously, unconsciously, or semiconsciously—our karma, which combines character, fate, and destiny into the outcome of our own handiwork. We are—and can be—the masters of our entire domain, whether we know it or not. Getting our hands on the steering wheel of our lives through understanding karmic cause and effect, conditioning, and interconnectedness is a major facet of the key to the wise and mindful, loving and altruistic, enlightened life. Thomas Bien's book helps provide the tools and techniques we need to concentrate, which some have called the root of education, and to attend to what needs to be done to achieve the goal of happiness on both the temporary and ultimate levels.

If you're not on the "happy bus" to satisfaction and well-being, why not get off and find another vehicle? An old Buddhist monk in ancient China probably said what we've all heard but have difficulty turning our minds to actually doing: it depends on whether you look at the half of the glass that's full or the half that's empty, which is mainly up to you.

What kind of positively insightful wisdom do we need to find to have the happiness and fulfillment, joyous ease, and well-being we long for so badly, almost universally? What is the direct route to health and healing, as well as physical and metaphysical well-being? Read this extraordinary book along with me and my friends, and find out!

—Lama Surya Das
Dzogchen Center
Cambridge, Massacusetts
Spring 2010

Lama Surya Das (www.surya.org) is a leading spokesperson for American Buddhism, and an authorized lama in the Tibetan Buddhist lineage. A translator, poet, meditation master, and spiritual activist, he is author of the best seller *Awakening the Buddha Within: Tibetan Wisdom for the Western World* and twelve other books, as well as numerous articles and publications, and in 1991 founded the Dzogchen Center and Dzogchen Center Retreats. Affectionately called "the American Lama" by the Dalai Lama, Lama Surya Das is a regular columnist at Beliefnet.com and the Huffington Post.

Acknowledgments

What is a book? If we speak of the physical object in the light of interbeing, a book is something that contains everything else. It contains the sunlight and the rain, the soil and the forest, the people who make the paper and the printer, and ultimately everything else. Without these things, the book in your hands cannot be.

Today a book can even exist without a physical form, as bits of data or pixels on a screen. When we look into a book in this form, we see that it contains ideas, sentences, and paragraphs. These originate ultimately in the author's experiences.

In either form, a book like this one contains the inspiration of many teachers. I am thankful for the life and teaching of Thich Nhat Hanh. I am grateful for the foreword from Lama Surya Das, a wonderful teacher and author. Some of my most important teachers are my clients, the wonderful and appreciative ones, as well as those who are more challenging.

A book also contains the network of the author's relationships. My wife Beverly and my son Joshua remain the constant stars in my firmament.

I am grateful to all at New Harbinger who invested so much time and energy in this book. Jess Beebe was invaluable at keeping the structure of the chapters clear. And without the efforts of Julia Kent and everyone in the marketing department, this book might not have ended up in your hands. Nelda Street performed an invaluable service with her careful copyediting. And a special note of gratitude goes to Catharine Sutker for her constant faith in this project.

Finally, let me thank you, gentle reader, for bringing yourself to these pages, interacting with them, and letting them touch you in any way that promotes your healing.

Introduction

Once during a difficult period in my life, a monarch butterfly fluttered past my window. When I saw that butterfly, I somehow knew—everything was going to turn out all right. Now, whenever summer comes around and I see that kind of butterfly again, I remember that happiness is always possible.

Our butterfly of happiness is always there, but how can we find it? If we try to catch the butterfly, if we try to clutch or grasp at the experience of happiness, we destroy the very thing that is our source of joy. Though such an approach is always tempting, it never actually helps.

At times of major loss or struggle, happiness can seem remote, abstract, and even unimaginable. It's as though life exists in different compartments. When we are living in the compartment of loss and grief, we can scarcely even imagine the compartment of happiness and well-being. Despair and cynicism can all too easily become entrenched in us so that we swiftly discount positive experiences, discrediting them the moment they arise, if they register at all, while we accept negative experiences unquestioningly.

But, important as they are, times of great loss and difficulty aren't the whole story. A lot of our unhappiness hinges on the petty difficulties and nuisances of daily life. At times, we can rise to the occasion and meet the challenge of great loss or the threat of a major problem. But the minor things gnaw at us: when we can't find a parking space, when we're forced to plod through computerized phone-answering systems, when rain derails our exercise plans, or when we find a mistake on a bank statement.

All of us seek happiness, but the ways we go about it often lack wisdom. Our ways of seeking happiness take on a life of their own. We lose perspective. We have no idea where we're going, but external forces and internal habits push us where we don't want to go. We become like the man carried on the back of a runaway horse. When a bystander asks where he's going, the rider shouts, "Ask the horse!" Instead of taking the reins ourselves, we let our ways of seeking happiness run away with us.

We think that if some success makes us happy, then having a lot of success will make us even happier. We imagine that if having enough money is part of being happy, then having more will surely create bliss. Instead of working to support our well-being, we allow work to take over our lives, dominating our thoughts even in off-hours. Worse still, some of the things we imagine will bring satisfaction are completely wrongheaded to begin with. Angry people may imagine they can't be happy unless they exact revenge. But once they've taken revenge, they find it fails to yield the expected satisfaction. When we are caught up in an argument, the need to win feels like a matter of life and death. But no one really wins. For even if we do win, we still lose in another, more important sense if winning hurts the relationship. That kind of winning only creates more suffering, more isolation and despair.

As a young, intellectually inclined person, I used to think happy people were rather superficial. I equated intelligence with skepticism and even cynicism. Anything else seemed unintelligent. Gradually, I have come to appreciate being happy. I now see that being happy in the midst of the difficulties of human life is a wonderful art, a great accomplishment. Learning to be happy is perhaps the most important skill we can develop in life.

Buddhism and the Path to Happiness

How can we learn to be happy? To learn about happiness and well-being, we have many sources available to turn to: Psychology can help. Therapy can help. Books and workshops can help. At the same time, we should not neglect the great spiritual traditions of the world. These traditions were hammered out over centuries. They have survived the test of time. Some of the wisest and brightest people who ever lived reflected on and added to these traditions. Because spiritual traditions grew in times and circumstances different from our own, we can't simply apply them in their original form to our time and circumstances. But the fundamental struggles of human life haven't changed. It would be tragic to neglect these streams of wisdom, as if we were orphans in the universe who had to puzzle it all out from scratch on our own.

We can learn from every spiritual tradition. From Christianity we learn that grace is central; from Judaism the value of a moral life led in earnest, a life of service and good deeds; from Islam the value of surrender to God; from Hinduism, that we are not separate from the divine; and from Taoism the value of quietude and nonstruggle.

A spiritual tradition that's appropriate for helping us find happiness today needs to meet certain criteria. It needs to be humanistic, helping us unfold our human potential. In an age of science, it needs to be empirical, at least in the sense of being based on experience rather than authority. It needs to be nondogmatic to keep from creating more barriers and divisions in the world. And it needs to be psychologically grounded, helping us deal with our worries, sadness, and anxiety. Buddhism meets these conditions almost perfectly.

First, Buddhism has a strong humanistic element. For all his deep insight, the Buddha never claimed—and even explicitly denied—being a god. And since he's not a god, he reveals what's possible for all human beings. He did it; you can do it. This is a high estimation of human capability.

Second, Buddhism has an empirical attitude, offering practices and insights as ways of working, trusting you to see for yourself whether these methods lead to inner transformation. Teachings are offered in the spirit that since others have had this experience, so can you. If that doesn't happen, take another approach. Buddhism urges us not to take anything on blind faith, but to follow the recommendations and see for ourselves.

Third, Buddhism is relatively nondogmatic. The Buddha always stressed that his teaching be taken as skillful means rather than ultimate truth. It's a path to follow, not a dogma to defend. The Buddha said that we even have to let go of true teachings, let alone untrue ones. The third Zen patriarch even suggests we stop seeking truth, and instead just stop cherishing opinions. Holding a belief we think is right, along with the corollary that others' beliefs are wrong, already contains the seed of violence, and has caused much human misery. Because of this open understanding of the nature of spiritual insight, many people have been able to take up Buddhist practice without rejecting their own spiritual heritage.

And for that matter, people have taken up Buddhist practice without rejecting atheism or agnosticism. With Buddhists, belief in God is up to you. From a Buddhist point of view, whether or not you believe in God isn't important, for what you must do to be happy and free is the same with or without God. Buddhism has been described as "functionally agnostic," meaning that while Buddhist texts refer to gods in accord with the worldview of the time, our own practice and insight are what actually matters. Only our own practice and insight can liberate us from suffering and delusion.

Of course, faith in God or a supreme being may remain important to you, and you can easily integrate this into the approach of this book. But the Buddhist emphasis is on practice. You don't have to believe anything. You don't have to defend anything. Follow the trail of your own experience. If you want to be happy and free from suffering, do the practices. See for yourself.

Buddhism as Psychology

Sometimes Buddhists do things that appear religious. They wear robes, burn incense, bow before altars, and enact rituals, as in other religions. But the heart of the matter isn't in these cultic aspects. You could even say that Buddhism isn't a religion at all. In fact, Buddhism is not really an "ism" of any sort. "Buddhism" is a Western word that doesn't exist as such in Buddhist countries. Instead, what we call Buddhism is referred to in the East as simply the *dharma,* or *Buddha dharma,* meaning "the way" or "the teaching" of the Buddha.

In fact, you can legitimately view the dharma as a wise and ancient psychology. Like a clinical psychologist today, the Buddha was keenly interested in easing human suffering. After discovering the insight that freed him of sorrow, he spent the next forty-five years finding ways to show others how to reach this insight for themselves, in accord with their individual capacities and inclinations. In this book, I approach the dharma in just this sense, as a psychology.

This book will show you how the Buddha's insights can help you be happy. You don't have to become Buddhist to find them helpful. They can help you deal with difficult emotions, loss, illness, and other troubles. They can even help you face death with wisdom and grace.

Chapter 1 explores the insights of the dharma to investigate some of our fundamental ideas and assumptions about happiness that tend to leave us disappointed, if not despairing. Chapter 2 challenges the conceptual traps that leave us imprisoned in sorrow and unhappiness. In particular, it reveals how the Buddha's insights can liberate us from the notions of permanence and separateness, which create much of our misery. Chapter 3 teaches how to work with the energy of habit so that it no longer dominates us. Since much of our unhappiness has to do with what we think and feel, chapter 4 provides insight into transforming our thoughts and feelings so that they no longer interfere with our capacity for happiness. Chapter 5 helps us deal with our relatedness both to ourselves and to other people. The Buddha's insight of no self, first described in chapter 2, provides the key to looking at this in a new way.

Chapter 6 examines the issue of our sorrow and suffering, and teaches why it can't be separated from the issue of our happiness. Chapter 7 offers exercises and concrete approaches for practicing happiness and well-being. It stresses that happiness involves more of an underlying attitude than any sort of contrivance. Chapter 8 offers a perspective on how living happily might look in daily life. And finally, chapter 9 gives us a glimpse into Buddhist insights on the ultimate nature of life and death.

From time to time, I have included examples from my work as a psychologist. While this material is realistic and based on actual experience, it's not based on particular individuals. Instead, these examples are composites.

How to Read This Book

I have written this book in an atmosphere of peace and nonstruggle, to help free all of us from suffering, to help us find happiness and well-being. Please read it in a peaceful way. Don't struggle. Take your time. Let the insights penetrate you easily and gently. Anything you find difficult now may make more sense at a later reading.

Read this book not necessarily to find happiness, but with a sense that happiness and peace are already present. For there's no way to happiness: happiness *is* the way.

chapter 1

Being Happiness

From joy springs all creation.
By joy it is sustained.
Toward joy it proceeds.
And to joy it returns.

—Mundaka Upanishad

Are you happy? Unless we're completely miserable at the moment, most of us would respond affirmatively. "Yes," we say, "I'm happy." But often we do so automatically, without reflecting on the matter. If we consider the question more deeply, the answer isn't so easy. The truth is more complicated, multifaceted. We may be happy in our careers, but unhappy in our primary relationships. We may be happy with our leisure time, but suffering miserably through our work hours. We may be happy with our sex lives, but unhappy with our bank statements. Moreover, even within these categories, the answer isn't as simple as a mere yes or no. There are aspects of our relationships we are happy with, others that are unsatisfying. There are aspects of our work lives we like, but others that worry us.

Often, too, we confuse the belief that we *should* be happy with the reality of our actual experience. Bumper-sticker wisdom says a bad day fishing is better than a good day at work, but if we look closely, it isn't always so. There are bad elements in what are otherwise pleasant recreational activities, and good elements in our work lives. Often, the idea that we're happy when it's the weekend and unhappy when it's the workweek doesn't hold up under examination. When we look closely, we discover that the reverse is often true. When we are present to our actual experience, we might find our sense of accomplishment at work more satisfying than the unstructured time of an uneventful weekend—just the opposite of what we frequently imagine.

If you stop amid your various activities and ask yourself, "Am I happy?" (an exercise I heartily recommend), you might be surprised at the answer. Sometimes you're happy doing things you normally consider less pleasant to do, and unhappy doing things you normally consider pleasant. More often than you imagine, you won't even know whether or not you're happy, or your feelings may be mixed.

Subtle signs appear when you are not as happy as you imagine. If you find yourself thinking a lot about some future situation when you will achieve your dream of happiness, perhaps you aren't so happy right now. If you observe your stream of thoughts and feelings and find yourself worrying a lot about things that might happen in the future, you are experiencing unease in the present. If you're preoccupied with things that went wrong in the past, it's hard to be satisfied now. Sometimes, when you really look, you may find subtly pervasive feelings of dissatisfaction and emptiness— feelings you try to avoid by running after whatever you can think of running after. Sometimes almost anything will do.

Human beings have been considering these things for a long time. In fact, it turns out that the question of happiness is a very old one.

Long Ago and Far Away

Some twenty-five hundred years ago, a young man sat at the base of a tree in northern India. His skin was deep brown from exposure to the hot sun, his beard and hair matted and unkempt. The rags he wore barely concealed his skeletal frame.

The young man's name was Siddhattha Gotama. Only a few years before, abrupt encounters with the harsh reality of human life had struck this sensitive and intelligent young man with savage force, leaving a profound existential wound. Afterward, he set out from his home of wealth and privilege, vowing not to rest until he found the answer to the predicament of human suffering, until he found the way to end it. That was now his single-pointed intention. To this end, he studied with some of the greatest spiritual teachers of his day, mastering their teachings with relative ease. And while these teachings were helpful, he remained unsatisfied. He still didn't know the answer. For the sake of other beings and himself, he was determined to find the way. And his determination was strong.

He had lived the life of an extreme ascetic, barely attending to basic bodily needs of food, water, and shelter, holding on to life by the thinnest of threads. But on this particular day, he accepted a cup of milk and a handful of rice. It amazed him how much better he felt! His mind was so much clearer. It was so much easier to meditate with a bit of nourishment. He vowed never to treat his body so harshly in the future. And with greater determination than ever, he vowed not to move from his spot beneath the tree until he found the answer.

That night, he received the breakthrough he had longed for. It changed him. From then on, when people met him, they knew they were in the presence of a remarkable person. They asked him, "Are you a divine being? Are you a saint or an angel?" but he denied being anything of the kind. When they then asked what he was, he merely responded, "I am awake (*buddh*)." And forever after, people called him Buddha, the Awakened One. It's said that when he got his breakthrough that night, the earth shook to its foundations.

What was it that Siddhattha had come to understand? His happiness was so striking that, in addition to being known as Buddha, he was also known as *Sugata*, the Happy One. What can he tell us about how to end our suffering and find well-being? What can he tell us about being happy? In essence, he shows us that, when we remove certain erroneous views we have of the nature of reality, happiness shines forth. Here and in the chapters that follow, we will look together at the Buddha's insights and how they can help us transform our suffering and find happiness.

Here and Now

Driving on the interstate recently, I spotted a billboard that revealed a lot about our idea of happiness. The billboard featured someone resting in a hammock with two bottles of Coke. The text read simply, "Open Happiness."

This advertisement shows that our idea of happiness has something to do with relaxing. And that's not a bad place to start. But it's also an ironic place to start, since most of us do so little of it. Most of us are better at doing and accomplishing than at taking it easy. This is so much the case that even when we finally have time to relax, we find it difficult to actually do so. After so much doing, we find it hard to have any sort of calmness or peace. Our bodies remain on alert, full of tension, our minds worried and restless.

We simply cannot run around frantically all day and then suddenly relax, unless it's just to crash from exhaustion.

Sometimes we try to relax by watching movies or television, or reading novels or magazines. This at least lifts us out of our usual preoccupations. But generally we expose ourselves to these media indiscriminately, and our bodies and minds become stressed by the very experience we use to try to relax. To truly relax involves just being. And we're not very good at that.

If the billboard captures an element of truth in the idea that happiness is related to relaxing, it's obvious nonsense that happiness will come to us in a bottle of anything. Commercialism and consumerism leave us empty. We would scarcely be taken in at all by this notion if we stopped and thought about it for a moment. Subtle advertising messages can only affect us if they slip in sideways while we're not really paying close attention. The idea that some product will make us happy doesn't survive even cursory examination.

Happiness Is Available

The billboard implies another message: happiness is found outside ourselves; if we can only acquire the right things and use or consume them, find the right people and be with them, get the right job, find the right psychotherapy, have enough money, and many other such schemes, we will be happy. Some of these things may be pleasant and even helpful, but the underlying implication—that happiness is found outside ourselves—is destructive.

How then do you find happiness? First, by realizing that happiness is always available. The moment you see the truth of this, you can be happy right away. You don't need to do anything else. You don't need to go anywhere else. You don't need to reform yourself or become a different person. Happiness is very simple. It's only our tendency to complicate things that makes it difficult.

Happiness is simple because ultimate truth is simple. When Christ says, "The kingdom of heaven is within," when the prophet hears God tell him to be still and know, we can't believe that's all there is to it. "All religions have come into existence because people want something elaborate and attractive and puzzling," comments the Hindu sage Ramana Maharshi (Mitchell 1991, 147). We have to add all manner of complications. We must have the correct belief. We have to follow certain rules. And all of this only obscures the fundamental truth, sometimes to such a degree that religion often insulates us from the lightning insight of awakening instead of facilitating it.

And it isn't just religion that makes happiness complicated; we manage to do this in many other ways as well. Many of the ways we go about seeking happiness only make it more difficult to find, and even prevent us from finding it.

Happiness is always available. This means, first of all, that you *can* be happy, right now, just as you are, in whatever circumstances you find yourself. There's nothing that needs to happen first for you to be happy. There's nothing that has to be added, subtracted, or changed. You don't have to be someone else. You can be happy right now.

Since happiness is always available, the real question is whether *you* are available to happiness. As the Upanishads (see chapter 2) tell us, joy is the underlying nature of things. You don't have to manufacture it. You need only remove the obstacles, including your unexamined concepts about happiness. When you learn to be available to happiness, these obstacles vanish. You immediately see that there's already enough, right here and right now, for you to be happy.

There's already enough happiness at hand. Consider our everyday human senses and capacities. You already have eyes that open you to the realm of wonderful forms and colors, ears that open you to the realm of beautiful sounds. You have two good hands, capable of doing many helpful and wonderful things. You have legs and feet that afford you the pleasure of walking, of contacting the earth joyfully with each step. You have a wonderful human mind with its almost mystical capacity for language. These are already incredible sources of joy. Even those of us who lack one or more of these capacities can still find rich sources of happiness in the remaining ones if we learn to appreciate them.

Happiness isn't something that's only for other people. The capacity to be happy is in you already. It isn't the sole right of special people, of people with the right genes, the right connections, the right looks. Often, what blocks you most from being happy is the idea that you don't deserve it. But deserving is only a concept. It's not about deserving or not deserving. Happiness simply is.

Finally, because happiness is always available, you can be happy *right now*. In fact, now is the only time you *can* be happy. The Buddha taught that the past is gone and the future is not yet here. The only time you can be alive is now. Now is when life is available. Do you believe you had happiness at some time in the past, but now it's unavailable? The past is gone. Happiness isn't available in the past. If you want to enjoy a refreshing glass of cool water, now is the only time you can do it. You can't drink the water of yesterday. The source of true happiness is the good and nurturing things around you and within you right now.

Do you think you will be happy in the future? The future isn't here. The future is *never* here. You can't be happy in the future any more than you can enjoy tomorrow's glass of water. If you don't know how to be happy in this moment, you won't be happy in the future either. The refreshing water that's available to you isn't a future glass of water any more than it's a past one. Both the future and the past are insubstantial images, hollow and empty, mere clouds and shadows. The past is a ghost, the future a dream. The water of life is available to you, in all its concrete and vivid reality, but only here and only now.

The idea that we can only be alive in the here and now is profound. But unfortunately, we rush past this insight as if it were obvious and not terribly interesting. But to grasp this insight fully, with clear understanding, is to be happy. We become available to life, and life becomes available to us. Taken superficially, as just a concept, the idea of living in the now offers little help. But if we take it as a practice, as a way of life, we can open to the experience of drinking this delicious water. And when we are present, when our awareness isn't squandered on what comes next or what came before, we are fully alive.

To put an end to suffering was the Buddha's only goal. He wasn't interested in starting a religion or a philosophy, or in speculating about metaphysical truth. He wanted only to end human suffering. To end suffering means to find happiness. To understand how this is so, to catch a glimpse of what the Buddha discovered on that night long ago, we need to understand the true nature of happiness.

Understanding Happiness

The chief obstacle to our happiness is our concept of happiness. Above all, we tend to think certain conditions must be present for us to be happy. We think we can't be happy until we meet certain life goals. All of this future-oriented thinking, instead of making us happy, becomes a reason for us to be unhappy now. And if we aren't happy now, the postponement of our happiness regresses into an infinitely receding future. We chase the horizon in endless anticipation and continual frustration. We never get there, because we always hope to arrive there *someday*. It's as if we are on a beautiful hiking trail, where there are spectacular mountains, lush meadows, cool streams, quiet lakes, and beautiful trees, but we're unhappy because we're caught in the concept that the view around the next corner will be better, while the one surrounding us now is nothing at all.

Rather than being about fulfilling certain conditions, happiness is about being receptive, about opening to what's good in the present moment—here, now, and this. When we are receptive, we know every moment that wonderful healing and nourishing things surround us. The song of the birds on my walk is nothing less than astonishing, but only if I am present and open. The white rose on the dining-room table is startling in its beauty, but only if I actually see it.

The Declaration of Independence asserts our right to pursue happiness, but the *pursuit* of happiness makes us crazy. We have struggled to be happy all our lives, but struggling is not finding. The idea that happiness is something to chase after deprives us of life and liberty, our other inalienable rights, and deadens us to the wonders of life that are here now. Like a dog chasing its own tail, we run in swift and vicious circles. But no matter how fast we run, we never reach the goal.

Consider a typical weekday morning. The blaring alarm clock jolts you from sleep, causing you to wake up already resisting the day, preferring to pull the covers over your head for just a few more minutes of sleep. Realizing it's a workday, you review all the stuff you have to do that day. As the list lengthens, you resist the day even more. You are barely aware as you go through your morning routine. The warm water of the shower is there, but you're not there for it. The smell of your coffee is there, but you barely notice it. Showering, you're already thinking about getting dressed and what you'll wear. Drinking your coffee, you're already rehearsing your problems, worries, and difficulties. Driving to work, you're struggling with the traffic, missing the beautiful morning sun, the clouds, the trees, and the sky.

Once we get to work, life is even more difficult. If we check in with ourselves at work, often we find ourselves entirely removed from the moment, rushing through each task just to get it done and get on to the next one. While doing one task, we're already thinking several items ahead on the lengthy list of things to do. We worry. We worry whether we can do it all. We worry whether our work will be appreciated. We worry whether our supervisor and coworkers like us. We can't wait for the day to be over. We become very tired, but it isn't the work that exhausts us. It's the getting ahead of ourselves, pushing impatiently into the future, all the fretting and worrying.

Even while driving home, we're impatient to arrive. Yet when we finally get there, we aren't really present. We're thinking ahead to the evening's activities. Or we're reviewing the workday. All this time is wasted, because in the midst of it all, we are fully awake, alive, and present in few, if any, moments. This kind of habit is strong in us.

The way to be happy in this situation is simple, but we often forget it. The way to be happy is to be fully available to the warm shower water, your coffee, and the birth of the day. You know that your worries are there, but you don't get lost in them. You don't disqualify yourself from life. You take each task one at a time. You allow yourself to be present during the drive home. You enjoy your evening.

As children, we knew how to be in the present moment. We enjoyed our breakfast. We noticed the rain and the puddles. But a parent's voice called out, "Hurry up! You'll be late for school." And while it was necessary for us to learn to be on time, such experiences also created a habit energy that pushed us endlessly into the future—a future that we would also miss. Now, as adults, we don't enjoy our breakfast. The puddles are just obstacles in our path.

In Buddhist cosmology, there's a type of being known as a "hungry ghost" (*preta*). These beings have large bellies, indicating great appetite, and small, pinhole-sized mouths and throats, indicating small capacity. Such beings are a good depiction of how we often live. We want and want and want. We want so much! We want without end and are never satisfied. Even in the abundance of developed nations, we remain perpetually frantic for more—not because we really lack, but because we have lost the capacity to be open, to receive and to enjoy what's there.

Happiness has less to do with what we have than with our capacity to be present. Happiness is about opening, receiving, learning to relax, letting that tiny mouth and throat open up fully to enjoy everything. Happiness is letting in what's happening.

Happiness Is Being Mindful

There are different kinds of happiness. There's the happiness of going on a special trip. There's the happiness of accomplishing or creating. And there's the happiness of achievement. While these can all be good things, the positive feelings that attend them are temporary.

The practice of learning to be happy and aware in the present moment is what the Buddha called "mindfulness" (smṛti). It's a stable kind of happiness, a happiness we can rely on because it contains calmness and contentment. It's reliable because it depends on our own intention, not conditions and circumstances. Mindfulness is about being awake in the moments of our lives, so that we don't come to the end of life and realize we missed it, that we missed the whole thing, because we were always somewhere else and somewhen else. Some elements in the present moment may be difficult for us, to be sure. But by closing ourselves off to those elements, we miss the miracles around us.

Happiness Isn't Excitement

Someone once told me that mindfulness isn't very exciting. He's right. For mindfulness is about contentment. It's about relaxing, calming, opening. Mindfulness is about ending our addiction

19

to things that, while exciting, leave us empty and dissatisfied in the end. That's why mindfulness is a solid foundation for happiness.

The happiness of the Buddha runs deep and has little to do with exhilarating experiences. It's the happiness of being deeply present and appreciating a flower growing out of a cranny in an old wall. Without the elements of calmness and contentment, of peace and ease, we can't be present. We miss the flower.

The moment you receive a wonderful promotion, get accepted to graduate school, start a wonderful new career, or meet your life partner is a pleasant moment. But because such moments contain the element of excitement, the experience fades quickly. The brain is simply not designed to stay in an excited state very long, but seeks to return us to a state of balance—a process called homeostasis. Whenever something wonderful and exciting happens, if you are mindful, you can enjoy it more fully, but you can also enjoy it when it's not so exciting anymore, when life returns to normal. When you are mindful, normal life contains wonders.

True happiness steals upon you quietly. It arrives when goals and projects have departed. It arrives when both excitement and boredom have left. You turn a corner and notice the sun streaming into the room, and a feeling of well-being and quiet joy arises. Seeing the green leafiness of an ordinary houseplant can give you a deep contentment. Simply eating lunch can be a time of deep happiness if you are really there, present to your food, your surroundings, and the people around you. But if you only talk and think about difficulties during lunch, you miss lunch. You can only enjoy these things if there's some stillness in you, if you aren't preoccupied. You can enjoy the streaming light, the green plant, and your lunch, but only if you are receptive. That's the single prerequisite.

Being Available to the Flower

One morning, the plant in my garden pond displayed an incredible orange blossom for the first time. This simple thing caused a feeling of quiet, deep happiness to arise in me. I wasn't seeking anything else as I stood before it, breathed and smiled, and opened myself to the experience of this beautiful and delicate flower. I could be happy in that moment because I was available to happiness.

You can do this. The light and radiance are in you. Happiness and peace are in you. Don't go running after it. Open to it—right now, right where you are. Smile.

Not Wasting Time

Our culture teaches that we shouldn't waste time. This means we should always be doing something productive; we should always be accomplishing something.

But when we know the nature of deep happiness, the kind of happiness the Buddha offers us, wasting time takes on a different meaning. We waste time when we're not present and open. It matters less what the activity is. Sitting and doing nothing may be valuable if we're open, aware, and alive, whereas reading a book can be a waste of time if we're not present to it, if we're just rushing through the process to finish and be done with it.

We have this valuable human life. Some Buddhists teach that we go through millions of lifetimes in other forms, in the hell realm, the animal realms, the realm of hungry ghosts, and even the realms of gods, all for the opportunity to acquire a human life. Only in a human life can we grow, becoming kind, happy, and wise. Only in this human life can we become awake, become a buddha. To waste this opportunity is to be unaware, to be asleep, closed, and unreceptive to what we're doing and what's going on.

Everything Is Best

One Zen student was frustrated by his lack of progress. He spent many hours meditating, but nothing happened. He remained unchanged and unhappy. One day he was sent to the market to buy food for the monastery. He told the shopkeeper he wanted only the best quality. "Everything is best!" replied the shopkeeper. And in that moment, the student became enlightened.

Realizing that everything is best means to stop judging everything, to stop focusing on the deficiencies of what's present and simply open to the experience itself. Everything is best when we stop comparing our experience to some imaginary ideal and realize that the experience of being alive is wonderful in itself. It's not that everything we see around us is perfect (which simply means the way we want it to be) but that the act of seeing itself is wonderful. It's not that the sounds around us are always pleasant but that hearing itself is amazing. Seeing, feeling, tasting, touching, smelling, and thinking are intrinsically satisfying and miraculous in their own right. It's not a matter of having everything just so. In fact, the need to have everything just so is what *prevents* us from being happy, prevents us from being fully alive and fully rooted in the moment of our experience. The quest for perfection, whether in our surroundings, our circumstances, or ourselves, wastes our time.

Not Struggling with Imperfection

As a young child considering a hangnail on my thumb in an otherwise pleasant moment, I saw that in life there always seemed to be something of this sort. Things never seem to be quite the way you want them to be. Maybe you got the birthday present you dreamed of getting, but it came without batteries. Maybe you have a wonderful bicycle to ride, but it has a flat tire. There always seems to be something naggingly imperfect in life. If you become obsessed with this imperfection, if you focus on it, it can completely dominate your consciousness. Even trying to avoid being aware of it only makes it worse, keeping you caught in the net. You become like someone trying to avoid noticing Cyrano's large nose. In the end, that nose is all you can think about.

The common thread in all of this is the element of resistance and struggle. We struggle with what's not perfect. Then we struggle against our struggling against it, which only multiplies the difficulty. We become sad, angry, or embarrassed, which wouldn't really be so bad, except then we also struggle against these emotional states. Being happy is about being able to relax into the imperfect nature of our experience, not about finally having everything just the way we want it. It's about being okay with imperfection.

Maybe When I'm Enlightened

Resistance to imperfection isn't just about external things. It's also about ourselves. In fact it's often *primarily* about ourselves, about the struggle between how we are now and how we think we should be. Even our noblest aspirations become just one more thing to interfere with enjoying the present moment. We have the idea that if we could only get it all together, attain some imagined state of complete wholeness and authenticity, everything would be great. Then we'd really be happy. Sometimes this idea isn't totally conscious, but can simmer in the background, influencing what we do and say, secretly creating discontentment and anxiety. Spiritual enlightenment is, for many, the ultimate version of this concept. But all such concepts, including enlightenment, can be obstacles that diminish our capacity to be open, accepting, aware, and alive.

The Buddha made a remarkable statement about his enlightenment. He said, "I obtained not the least thing from unexcelled, complete awakening, and for this very reason, it is called 'unexcelled, complete awakening'" (Watts 1957, 45). What an amazing thing to say. Why would he have said such a thing? There are several different ways we can approach his meaning.

For one thing, the Buddha wants you to know that enlightenment, as an idea or a concept, will only get in the way of your establishing the real thing. The idea you have of enlightenment is just an idea, far from the living reality. *Nirvana,* the term Buddhists use for an enlightened person's state of being, means "extinction." Rather than being about the extinction of who we are, this is about the extinction of our suffering. It's about the extinction of the concepts and ideas that interfere with our direct perception of the wondrous nature of things as they really are in their amazing reality, what Buddhists call "suchness" (*tathata*).

Ideas of psychological wholeness and well-being can also get in our way. A depressed person who aims to get rid of all sad thoughts and feelings will only become increasingly caught up in sadness. Checking assiduously to see whether we are meeting this ideal of no sad thoughts makes us attend to them even more. The idea that we can eliminate all sad thoughts is just an idea. It only makes us feel even more like a failure, causing more sad thoughts and depression, continuing the vicious cycle.

The Buddha's statement that he gained nothing from enlightenment reminds us that enlightenment comes from a different realm of experience. "*Gate gate paragate parasamgate bodhi svaha!*" is the mantra of the Heart Sutra (Thich Nhat Hanh 1988, 2), meaning "Gone, gone, gone beyond; gone completely beyond; hail enlightenment!" This kind of consciousness is a crossing over to another shore. What was foreground becomes background, and what was background becomes foreground. Enlightenment is a state of mind where our conditioning, including our goals and dreams, doesn't push us around. Even if our goals and dreams are wonderful, even if they are both healthy and reasonable, they have a downside: they pull us away from the present moment. Making enlightenment our goal (or wholeness, perfect well-being, or anything of this kind) in the same sense we make a goal of other things just creates another problem. This isn't fundamentally different from concentrating on more mundane goals, and is in some ways worse, for being an unquestioned good makes it even more insidious. We place something else between ourselves and our happiness. Once we do that, we strain after the goal, trying too hard, pushing and forcing.

Searching is not finding. Trying too hard is antithetical to peace, and thus antithetical to enlightenment. opposite

So the Buddha teaches us that if we think of enlightenment as a goal like other goals, or if we take it as a concept without realizing that even the most refined concept is still a concept, we'll get caught. Enlightenment is a *nongoal*. Enlightenment is about what Buddhists call "goallessness" or "aimlessness" (*apranihita*). It has more to do with being present with and accepting things the way they actually are, without distorting them through desire or aversion.

The same is true of happiness. Making happiness a goal only complicates things. Don't practice mindfulness to be happy. Don't set out to become a buddha. Just come back to the present moment, to your body and mind, and let your buddha nature shine forth. Touch the happiness that already is.

Not Gaining

The Buddha said he gained nothing from total enlightenment because total enlightenment isn't about gaining. It certainly isn't about acquiring some *thing* called enlightenment. Nirvana stands outside the realm of gain and loss. It isn't something to carry in your pocket. It isn't a commodity to trade on the market. You can't put it on your résumé.

The way out of the trap is always about simply relaxing into the present moment. The way out is to realize you already are what you aspire to be. Your aspiration already sets in motion processes that lead you gently where you intend to go, that in fact already express in the moment what you want to be. Humanistic psychologist Abraham Maslow said it well: "The human being is simultaneously that which he is and that which he yearns to be" (Maslow 1968, 160). The Buddhist way of saying this is that you already have buddha nature within you. And therefore, spiritual practice isn't about trying to become something you aren't, forcing yourself to be something else, but about removing the obstacles to what you already are.

Why Your Dog Is Happier Than You Are

When you watch a dog play, it's difficult not to smile. Dogs enjoy everything. Give them their food and water, and they're happy. Pat them on the head, and they're happy. Scratch them behind the ears, they're happy. The merest mention of the word "walk" triggers ecstasy.

Perhaps they're happy because they don't think so much. For us, on the other hand, it's quite different. This large brain costs us so much to own and operate, using something like a third of our metabolism. It's so important to our survival that our bodies protect it with a hard, bony skull. With this big brain, we can create symbols: numbers and words, ideas and metaphors. We can, in turn, manipulate these symbols as though they were the actual things, at times with astounding results.

But it's important to remember: these symbols are not the actual things. Forgetting this causes no end of mischief. Because of our tendency to treat the symbol as reality, if someone speaks certain words to us, or even makes certain gestures, it triggers a strong emotional reaction in us. Feelings of sadness, anger, shame, or other painful states arise. We can get very upset about this, and that feeling can continue for hours or even days. It continues as we then rehearse the same symbols mentally: *He said this to me. She did that to me. How could she do that? How could he say that?* We try to solve the problem by inventing clever rebuttals and comebacks, but this attempt at resolution only feeds the process, further entrapping us.

During the stand-up comedy segment of an episode of *Seinfeld*, Jerry contemplates why displaying the middle finger elicits such strong emotion. By pointing to the arbitrariness of this gesture, he helps us see that this symbol is only a symbol. No actual harm is done to us. Through Jerry's eyes, we see that this situation is actually quite laughable. In the same way, if we confuse our symbols with reality, they will often deepen our suffering and unhappiness.

One time, the Buddha was confronted by someone who cursed him to his face. When the Buddha didn't respond, the person cursed him even more vehemently for not responding. Eventually the man could only give up in frustration. Later, the Buddha's followers asked about the incident. How could he remain calm during such an awful attack? The Buddha only commented that when a gift is not received, the giver must take it back. The Buddha knew there was nothing to get upset about in the symbols and words the man used. Ultimately, they're only sounds. They have no more meaning than the wind.

Manipulating symbols is also part of the process of how we get stuck in thinking about the past or future. Thinking about the past or future is a symbolic process. And while it's one thing to reflect on the past to make sense of it, or anticipate the future to plan for it, it's quite another thing to get lost in the past or future. When we do that, it's like trying to clutch at water. Life itself slips through our grasp.

Don't Get Caught in Words and Ideas

The Buddha knew that language gets in the way of our being happy. Instead of letting language point to direct experience, we get caught up in the words themselves. He even applied this insight to his own teaching, something unique among spiritual traditions.

In the Sutra on the Better Way to Catch a Snake, the Buddha uses three comparisons to reveal the nature of spiritual teaching: he says his teachings are like a raft, like a finger pointing at the moon, and like picking up a poisonous snake.

First, the teachings are like a raft someone uses to cross a stream. After using it, it makes no sense to then lug the thing around on your head as some kind of prized possession. The raft has accomplished its purpose. Leave it behind. Leave it by the water for someone else to use. The purpose of the teaching, in other words, is to get you across to the other side, from the shore of sorrow to the shore of happiness and well-being. The raft itself isn't to become an object of worship or veneration.

The Buddha also compared his teachings to a finger pointing at the moon. Someone who's pointing to the moon wants you to see the moon, not stare at the pointing finger. The teaching exists to show us how to look, how to have a different and deeper perception of what is. The teaching isn't there to fixate on. Far too often, the world has witnessed the conflict and heat of people who rigidly hold on to teachings—or at least their view of the teachings— defending them aggressively and creating a lot of misery in the world. The Buddha doesn't want us to get caught in this trap.

Finally, the Buddha said his teachings are like picking up a poisonous snake. The right way to pick up a snake is to plant a forked stick down into the ground right behind the snake's head. Then you can pick up the snake in the same place with your hand. In this way, no matter how much it writhes and wriggles, the snake can't bite you. But if you pick it up by the tail, you get bitten. What's the right way to pick up the teachings of the Buddha? The right way is to learn so you can put them into practice, not to acquire knowledge to show off to others. The right way is to practice them as happiness.

Teachings can be dangerous. Invariably, given the structure of human thought and language, the teachings give the impression that there's a goal to reach. Buddhist teachings about different stages of practice, for example, can give us some idea of what may come along on the road ahead so that we know the path has been traveled by others. But unfortunately, talking about stages can make us anxious to reach the next stage, and then the next. It can make us dissatisfied with how we are now, and cause discouragement. This is the opposite of present-moment awareness. This is the opposite of happiness.

Continually assessing your progress is like pulling the beautiful flower in your garden out by the roots to see how it's doing. So while we may track our "progress," feel encouraged to realize that our capacity has grown and that we can now do something we couldn't do before, we need a lot of wisdom about this. Don't get bit! Remember that enlightenment isn't about gaining and that the practice is nonpractice. A goal orientation strangles the life out of spiritual practice. It strangles our happiness.

The Way We Search Prevents Us from Finding

It's good practice to count our blessings. It's good to be in touch with what's positive in our lives. The problem is, we can go about this practice in a forced, mechanical way, like a child doing arithmetic homework, devoid of energy and enthusiasm. When we approach this practice this way, is it any wonder that its effectiveness is limited, if it has any effect at all? The way we're going about it doesn't serve what we want to accomplish, unless it's done with joy.

Sitting at the dinner table as a child, you may have been admonished to finish your dinner because there were children starving in India. The intention behind such parental injunctions is good, but the effect often isn't. Instead of feeling grateful for your food, you probably just felt manipulated. So instead of coming to a deeper appreciation of your food, you may have only rebelled against the pressure. After all, quite young children can see that eating their lima beans ("Yuck!") won't help anyone far away. And rather than feeling grateful to have food to eat, they just become distressed.

If we bully ourselves like this, trying to be happy by forcing a sense of gratitude, is it any wonder we don't succeed? Sometimes people in psychotherapy treat themselves this way. They experience difficulties that they know are minor compared to the difficulties other people encounter: "What's my divorce compared to the suffering in Darfur?" "What's my unemployment compared to someone's terminal illness?"

Please be careful with this. It's good to take perspective on the size of our suffering, for this might serve to open our compassion. But include yourself in the circle of compassion too. Often we use this insight in a self-punishing way. Not only am I unhappy, but I'm also a terrible person for being unhappy since others have it so much worse! Use this insight, but not to treat yourself as though you yourself don't deserve kindness. Your suffering matters. Don't dismiss it. This won't give you happiness. It will only increase your pain.

When we think of these and other methods commonly used to find happiness, we have the chance to understand why the Buddha said his practice is nonpractice. By this, he means not going about practices like meditating, following precepts, and living mindfully as if they're something to get done as quickly as possible so you can get to the good stuff that comes later. Practicing gratitude for the good things in our lives, appreciating our food, and practicing meditation are all good things, but if we go about them in a joyless manner, the result won't somehow mysteriously become joyful.

The Way Things Really Are

The Buddha taught that we aren't happy because we have some profound misconceptions about the way the world is. Viewing ourselves as separate from the rest of life, we feel alienated and alone. Feeling separate from others makes it seem acceptable to treat others unkindly. Only when we release such distorted views can we see that the underlying nature of things is joy.

You're not isolated. You are profoundly interconnected with other human beings; with nonhuman beings; with the earth, the sun, and the whole universe. Everything in the universe has come together so you can be here, alive, present, and aware. In chapter 2 we explore this insight more fully.

Training in Happiness (Mindfulness)

Can we train ourselves to be happier? We can. But we must go about doing so with wisdom. If we go about it in a heavy-handed way, with a strict and rigid discipline, how can joy result from that? The means must resemble the ends. The ways we go about becoming happier must already contain happiness, or we won't succeed. The Buddha said that his way is pleasant in the beginning, pleasant in the middle, and pleasant in the end. The way to practice is to make the path pleasant.

Mindfulness is the practice of being happy in the present moment. Mindfulness means being aware of what's going on in an accepting way, opening ourselves to our experience. We stay in touch with what's good around us. When we practice mindfulness, we are practicing happiness in a simple, direct, and powerful way. Force, rigidity, and obsession won't help us.

Being mindful means to see things with the eyes of a poet to discover what's interesting and wonderful in the present moment. It isn't so much about seeing the flower as a botanist might, using cold intellect to dissect the different parts and their functions, but seeing the flower with the heart. Mindfulness sees the world as warm and alive. Mindfulness sees with kindness, insight, and compassion—for ourselves and for others.

Rebalancing Negative Perception

Evolution teaches us that living organisms evolve to survive and pass on their genes. The human brain also evolved that way. It evolved because it helps us survive. Because of its tendency to facilitate survival, the brain focuses more attention on what's wrong in our surroundings than on what's right. In terms of survival, it's more important to remember where the bear lives than to remember that sitting on a certain cliff at a certain time of day brings you a great view of the setting sun.

For this reason, the brain has a bad attitude. It's always scanning for what's wrong. But fortunately, we now know that the brain is *plastic*, meaning it can change. The human brain contains about a hundred billion neurons, while each neuron has something like ten thousand connections with other neurons. It's a living and dynamic process, not a static structure. It continually reshapes itself, making new connections between nerve cells. This is why we can learn to modify the negative, survival-based nature of our brains.

When we are mindful, we notice the wonders around us. Everything becomes clear and deep. And this is possible because we can learn to attend to what we want to attend to, instead of letting our genes or our conditioning compel us to continue in old patterns.

What we focus on becomes real. So while the news may reveal sad developments in the world or you may contend with sad developments in your own life, and you must remain in touch with these difficulties, through mindfulness you can also stay in touch with the positive, healing, and nurturing aspects of life. Attending to these gives you not only happiness but also the capacity to deal with your difficulties. Rather than being a matter of trying to force inflated feelings of happiness, it's about opening more to the happiness that's all around and within us, noticing what we normally don't notice. And there's so much there to notice!

Man on an Island

The Buddha always stressed that he was a human being. As a human being, he shows what human beings can do. He wants you to know that if he can do it, you can do it. Indeed, if he were a god, it would mean much less for our lives, since we live the life of human beings, not the life of gods. The humanity of the Buddha shows that it's possible for you to become someone who's happy, peaceful, kind, and wise.

In the Galleria dell'Accademia in Florence, you can see Michelangelo's astounding statue *David*. Though we've all seen photographs of it, standing before it is an experience. I'm not the only one I know whose eyes welled with tears at seeing it. But along the sides of the hall leading up to the *David* are a number of unfinished Michelangelo figures that are equally amazing in their own way. Each figure is incomplete. Each seems to be struggling to emerge from the stone that imprisons it.

That's exactly how Michelangelo understood his work as a sculptor. He didn't see himself as inventing a figure, bringing something to birth that didn't previously exist, but as *freeing* the figure already present in the marble. In the same way, you are already a buddha. It's possible to free the buddha within you—to be a happy person, a wise person, a kind person—because this is your essential nature. You need only remove the hindrances. You need only remove the stone that's in the way. In the words of Zen master Thich Nhat Hanh, "There is no one who does not have the capacity to be a Buddha.... Stop being like the man...who looked all over the world for the gem that was already in his pocket. Come back and receive your true inheritance. Don't look outside yourself for happiness. Let go of the idea that you don't have it. It is available within you" (Thich Nhat Hanh 1998, 175).

Enlightenment is like being on an island. You search frantically for something you lost, looking and looking and looking. You get desperate and frustrated. Then one day, you pause, relax a bit, and look around you. For the first time, you see that the island is beautiful.

———— Practice: ————
Open to Happiness

Take a long, deep look at a beautiful flower. As you breathe, be aware of each breath in and out. Without trying to grasp or analyze, simply see about opening yourself to the flower. As you look at it, breathe in and out a few times, saying to yourself, "calm," then "open," and then "beautiful." See if you can feel a sense of connection with the flower, a sense of oneness.

Repeat this exercise as often as you like. Notice how one time you may be more receptive, and another time, less so. You can also try this with other beautiful objects, like a tree, a mountain, a green leaf, or the blue sky. Practice in the spirit of nonpractice, remembering that the point is not to accomplish anything but just to be happy in the present moment, enjoying the flower, enjoying your own presence, awareness, and aliveness.

chapter 2

Releasing Concepts

The self is merely a locus in which the dance of the universe is aware of itself as complete from beginning to end—and returning to the void. Gladly. Praising, giving thanks, with all beings.

—Thomas Merton

If someone knocked at your door and told you, "The sky is raining cactus, and we're all going to die!" you might suspect this person to be suffering from delusions. You could easily see that the announcement didn't correspond to reality. You might sympathize with your visitor, while knowing that this person's terrible fear was based on an erroneous perception.

From the Buddha's perspective, you and I are a bit like the unfortunate person at the door. We, too, are deluded. Our suffering, too, is based on erroneous perceptions rooted in deeply ingrained concepts about the way things are. The difference between us and the person at the door is really not as great as we imagine. Let's take a look at what this means.

Concepts Are Dangerous

Zen Buddhism is the tradition of strange words and strange actions. One Zen master taught that whenever he said the word "Buddha," he had to wash his mouth out three times. Understanding what the teacher meant, one of his students added that, for himself, whenever he heard the word "Buddha," he had to wash his ears out three times. Such wild, iconoclastic teachers have been found doing things like burning statues of the Buddha or walking out of a room with their sandals on top of their heads. Zen master Lin-chi even said that if you meet the Buddha on the road, you should kill him.

These teachers are trying to make a point in a dramatic, unforgettable way. Through their irreverence, they want us to wake up to the fact that all our notions, all our ideas and concepts, are just that—notions, ideas, concepts. All of them pale before the wondrous becoming that is the true nature of reality. Trying to capture reality in concepts is like trying to grasp water in your hand. It's like trying to capture space with a net.

Concepts can be dangerous. People who wage war to gain land and property don't destroy the land and property, because that's what they're trying to acquire. But people who go to war in the name of concepts destroy everything. They want to wipe out ideas contrary to their own. It's for this reason that Communist China has been so savage in its treatment of Tibet, destroying precious and irreplaceable manuscripts and monasteries, imprisoning and torturing Tibetan monks and nuns for years on end, sometimes just for having a photograph of the Dalai Lama. The Chinese act in this ruthless manner because they are waging war against ideas.

They want to replace the ideas of Buddhism with the ideas of communism and materialism.

The more sacred the concept, the more dangerous it can be. Even a concept of the Buddha can become an idol. In reality, the Buddha is your capacity for peace, kindness, wisdom, and happiness. If we get trapped into thinking of Buddha as a reality outside of ourselves, we will never look where Buddha can actually be found. We become like someone who lost a set of keys in the shadows a mile away but searches for them under a nearby streetlight. The person knows the keys aren't under the light, but the light is better there. Though always available, Buddha can only be found in ourselves and in our own lives.

If we think of Buddha as something outside of ourselves, we'll always be rushing off to somewhere else. We imagine we'll find Buddha through a certain teacher or on a special retreat. But the Buddha to be found outside of yourself isn't Buddha at all. The only Buddha that counts is the one within you.

Courage to Let Go

Letting go of our concepts requires courage. It's shattering to release the comfort of familiar ideas. We feel we have no place to stand. Though our concepts limit us by cutting us off from reality and destroying any real chance of happiness, we cling to them because they give us some sense of a world that's comfortable, understandable, and predictable. When we stand before a beautiful old tree, it's as though we say to ourselves, "Yes, I know what that is. It's a thing called a tree. See here, it has a trunk. It has branches and leaves. Just as I thought, it's a tree." To see a tree that way is to see a dead thing. We only confirm what we already know, that this type of thing has a name and that it has certain predictable parts. But seeing in this way, we miss the miraculous living process before us.

One time Zen master Thich Nhat Hanh was giving a talk at a prison. A member of the audience noted that he sat quietly in meditation before the talk, ignoring the people present (Thich Nhat Hanh 2002). He found it remarkable that he could do this in the presence of more than 80 guests from around the world and over 120 inmates. But Thây (as the Zen master is called) was simply being himself, centered in the present moment. He wasn't caught in the concept of giving a talk. In the language of Zen, there was no one there called "teacher" doing something called "giving a talk." There was no one present called "audience" or "inmates." He wasn't hooked in the concept of a separate self. What this means will become clear later in this chapter.

Letting Go of Our Stories

We love to tell stories. While stories differ in content, their structure is predictable. A limited number of main and subsidiary characters are involved. Usually one of them is the main character, or protagonist, and we see the story largely through that person's eyes. A difficulty arises, a dangerous journey must be made, or a mystery must be solved. We have to move through the difficulty to the solution, so we can then return home. We can reach a place of resolution.

The story of the Buddha can be seen as a hero story. There's a difficulty that must be addressed (human suffering), a quest to be made, a solution to be found. We are so used to thinking of things this way that we seldom question this basic structure.

The Buddha, however, said little about himself or his story. He didn't feel that he, as a particular person, had any special importance. What was important to him was his dharma, his insight or teaching. Much to the frustration of biographers and historians, he left little record of his personal life in the *sutras*, the Buddhist records of his teaching. You can find a little information about his life before enlightenment and a little about his death. Much of what's recorded is the stuff of myth and legend more than biography or history as we understand the terms. Information about the bulk of his life and teaching career, the period between his enlightenment and his death, is relatively scarce. He clearly didn't want to be venerated, but wished to help people find what he had found. He wanted us to see that the realm of nonsuffering, the realm of happiness, is right here and now. The realm of nirvana is present if we open to it.

We get stuck in the drama of our lives. If we are to find happiness, we instinctively feel we have to go through something, endure some difficulty, go on a quest, slay dragons and monsters, and ultimately find the gold or the princess in order to find the resolution and peace we seek. When we are told that happiness is available right now, we can hardly escape thinking we have to do, endure, and struggle to find it. We almost can't help it.

Seeing life as "story" gets us caught in the notion that we don't have happiness. We have to *go after* happiness somehow. We have to achieve great wealth or fame. We have to acquire a lot of money. Needing to find enlightenment is the same thing. We feel we must endure great struggles and difficulties in our quest for it. It's so much a part of the structure of our awareness to think this way that we seldom consider questioning it.

"I don't have it. It's very difficult. I have to struggle for it." This is why we must wash our mouths when we say "Buddha," because we see even the Buddha in these terms. To become enlightened, we think of him as having practiced heroic discipline: he had to do dangerous and difficult things. But in reality, it was when he eased up, when he decided to work *with* his human nature rather than against it, that he slipped into the state he called nirvana. When he relaxed and opened, he found peace and happiness. When we learn that we can be happy right now, just breathing in and out, and seeing a leaf for the miracle it actually is instead of the idea of "leaf," we're almost disappointed. We want it to be a great achievement. If we can't find a way to see it as an achievement, then we can't feel special and feed the ego. Instead, in seeing things as they actually are, we step outside the ego.

The Story: I Don't Deserve to Be Happy

When the Dalai Lama began coming to the West, he met with a group of American meditation teachers. He was taken aback to learn that many people in the West have a negative view of themselves. At first, he thought it was a translation problem. He just didn't understand what he was hearing. The Tibetan language doesn't even have a term for low self-esteem. When he finally understood, he was shocked.

You can wonder what it is about our culture that makes so many of us suffer from low self-esteem. Maybe it's our religious heritage, which focuses too much on a fallen state and sin, an attitude that pervades our culture even when consciously rejected. Maybe there's something about how we parent our children. But part of the problem is also the concept of self-esteem itself. If you can have high self-esteem, then you can also have low self-esteem. If you have to struggle to cultivate self-esteem, then self-esteem is something you don't have, and something you can lose again once you do. And all of our apparent focus on ourselves and our individual happiness is ultimately a compensation for the fact that, in the end, we don't feel very good about ourselves. And since we don't feel good about ourselves, we can only imagine finding happiness by going through trials and difficulties that somehow establish our worthiness.

Buddhism can help us with our low self-esteem. But it can also help us with our high self-esteem. To appreciate this, we need to understand how radical the Buddha's insight was. We need to understand the profoundly different way he invites us to view life, so we can discover the happiness and well-being already present. His insight shows us that the whole idea of comparison is problematic, built on a false view of what we are, as will become clear a bit later in this chapter. But first, here's another kind of story.

The Story: I Can't Be Happy Because Others Suffer

Once, I attended a prosperity blessing given by some Tibetan monks who were traveling through town. The teacher spoke at length in Tibetan and then paused for one of the monks to translate his words into English. He talked quite animatedly for varying lengths of time, and the translator then summarized what he'd said. But no matter how long the teacher had talked, the translated summary was always something like, "He says, 'The most important thing is right intention.'" Right intention means selfless love for all beings.

Tibetan Buddhism emphasizes selflessness and kindness from beginning to end. It's part of the great Mahayana tradition in Buddhism, which views seeking enlightenment for yourself alone as a lesser goal. But when we practice with the intention of helping other beings, this changes everything.

Kindness and compassion are core practices in Buddhism. But often when I teach, someone raises an objection that we shouldn't feel peaceful because people in the world are suffering injustice. The topic of my talk might be living mindfully or practicing mindful psychotherapy, not social justice or peace work per se. But people become uneasy and raise this concern. It's a bit like attending a class on painting and questioning why we aren't talking about sculpting.

We somehow assume there's an antagonistic relationship between inner peace and outer peace. In reality, inner peace is the sure foundation of our work for outer peace, for service to others.

If we aren't peaceful, it will be difficult for us to be deeply present to others. If we aren't peaceful, we will speak and act unskillfully. We may well do more harm than good, antagonizing people rather than persuading them, causing them to harden their positions rather than open to dialogue. Inner and outer peace are inextricably connected.

Of course, our concern for peace and justice is important. But using it to refuse to allow ourselves to be happy returns us to a form of that parental guilt trip about how we should eat everything on our plates because of hungry children far away. Sometimes a feeling of unworthiness may underlie this attitude. Because we don't feel worthy, we think we don't deserve peace; we must not allow our unworthy selves to feel happy till everyone is happy.

Our happiness can't be separated from that of others, which is why we must do all we can to help. Yet at the same time, our happiness is the first and most important gift we can give to other people. If we aren't happy, we only contribute to the misery in the world every day through our actions and words.

Radical Release of Concepts

The Buddha encourages us to let go of our ideas so we can see things as they really are. In particular, he wants to help us let go of two ideas that profoundly skew our view of the world: the idea of permanence and the idea of self.

Releasing Permanence

The Buddha lived during a period of time historian Karl Jaspers called the Axial Age. It was a time of change and turmoil, and therefore a time when people were reaching for new answers. In ancient Israel, the Hebrew prophets thundered in the name of the Lord, declaring that you were not saved just because of your status as a Jew, but only if you were transformed inwardly. Being saved meant becoming the kind of person who cared for those in society who were least able to care for themselves.

In China, a man named Kung-tse, known to us as Confucius, was walking across a bridge. Seeing the water in the stream below, he said, "Flowing like this, day and night!" In ancient Greece, the philosopher Heraclitus made the same observation: "Everything flows!" Each was talking in his own way about the ever-changing and impermanent nature of reality. Both of these individuals, independently of each other, reached the same insight in the same era.

It was also a time of great change in India. Aryan horsemen invaded the plains of the Ganges. People lost faith in the ancient religion of the Vedas, whose rituals no longer seemed effective in providing help or protection. Instead, a radical new faith was forming. Its teachings became known as the Upanishads, a term based on Sanskrit words that mean "to sit side by side." For these teachings were transferred intimately, from teacher to student. The Upanishads taught that *atman* is *Brahman*, that the "self" within you is "God." In theological language, God immanent is God transcendent.

Like Confucius and Heraclitus, the Buddha also noted the impermanent nature of everything. Everything is impermanent. Nothing lasts. Everything is changing all the time. Nothing is the same from moment to moment. And this is so, not just in the sense of easily noticeable changes, such as when cool water comes to a boil or when someone dies, but also in the sense that, throughout the process of coming to boil, the water is changing, in the sense that every second, millions of blood cells are born while millions of others die.

Life and death co-occur in every moment, not just at the moment death becomes visible. Feelings and thoughts change every moment. Whatever arises is already in the process of ceasing. And what appears to be something static and unchanging, like a human being or a tree, is really change itself. Permanence is just an idea. It has nothing to do with reality.

But impermanence is more than an idea. It's an *insight*, an insight into the nature of reality. It's an insight with the power to liberate us from our sorrow. For while everyone knows, at least in a vague and abstract way, that everything is impermanent and changing, the Buddha could see in this insight something life changing and transformative.

Impermanence isn't a dogma. You don't have to take anyone's word for it. You can easily see it for yourself. Nor is impermanence pessimistic. It's neither pessimistic nor optimistic. It's simply what is. There are positive as well as negative aspects to impermanence. While it's true that, because of impermanence, we all will die, it also means that the hated political regime will one day come to an end. Because of impermanence, knowledge can replace ignorance, our children can grow into adulthood, and the orange blossom can transform into delicious fruit.

Life itself is made possible by impermanence. If we were permanent, we'd be like statues, cold and dead rather than warm and alive. The winter tree could never put forth leaves again. The rays of the sun would never reach the earth. Everything would be static and lifeless.

Impermanence isn't the cause of our suffering. We don't suffer because things are impermanent. We suffer because we don't *like* that the nature of things is impermanent. We refuse to accept what's obviously true. We suffer because we fight against this reality. And when we fight against reality, reality always wins— every time.

To be happy, we need only stop resisting what is. It may seem difficult to accept this, but it's actually far more difficult not to accept it. We suffer so much from change and loss because they always surprise us, as though we didn't know they could happen or at least that they could happen to us. But when we see that everything is marked with impermanence, we can stop the struggle. We can come to appreciate the way things really are. And the way things really are is the way of impermanence, the way of wondrous becoming, everything altogether unfolding all at once.

To be happy is to accept with openness and serenity the impermanent nature of things. Everything is flowing and changing all the time. There's nothing to cling to. The cosmos is a great, swirling dance of creation and destruction.

Join the dance.

Releasing Self

If we resist the insight of impermanence, the Buddha's insight about the self can give us serious pause. His view of the self is radical, in the sense of going to the root of the issue, to the root of our unhappiness. According to the ancient records, it was this insight that caused a number of those who heard the Buddha to become enlightened on the spot, permanently leaving their unhappiness behind. Whether or not that's historically accurate, through such accounts we can see the high value placed on these insights for transformation, for the release from suffering, and for our happiness and well-being.

The Buddha proposed that if you look deeply into your own experience, you won't find anything there to call a self. There's no homunculus inside us pulling the strings. All you can be aware of is your body and its sensations, and your mind and its thought processes. But where, in any of that, is there a self?

Neuropsychologist Rick Hanson (2009, 211) agrees:

In sum, from a neurological standpoint, the everyday feeling of being a unified self is an utter illusion: the apparently coherent and solid "I" is actually built from many subsystems and sub-subsystems over the course of development, with no fixed center, and the fundamental sense that there is a subject of experience is fabricated from myriad, disparate moments of subjectivity.

When you look deeply, you see that you are composed entirely of nonself elements. While reading this sentence, you're exchanging matter and energy with the environment around you. When you eat, what was nonself a moment ago is now self. When you breathe in, molecules that were not self become self. When you breathe out, air molecules that were self are no longer self. When you use the toilet, matter that was self is no longer self.

What are you then, if you aren't a separate self? You are the sunlight. You are the earth. You are the water. All that you are can be traced to these things. You are not a static self, not something separate from everything else, but a dynamic life process, deeply interrelated with everything else around you and in the entire cosmos. Innumerable causes and conditions have come together for you to manifest. Remove any one of them, and you're no longer there, for you are not separate from these causes and conditions. In fact, you're not separate from anything.

We can understand nonself against the background of Hindu belief and practice in the Buddha's time. The deepest truth of Hinduism, as mentioned previously, is that atman is Brahman; that is, the self is the Godhead. The Buddha meditated for years to try to find the atman within him, but he couldn't do it. It was only when he gave up the quest in exhaustion and relaxed that he had the realization: there's no such thing as a self! And at this point, he left sorrow behind and entered the happiness of nirvana.

This initially disturbing idea holds the key to liberation. When you come to see that you aren't a separate self, then the idea that you are or aren't a valuable person, the idea that you have or don't have self-esteem, is revealed for what it is: simply an idea, an event arising temporarily in your consciousness. Such thoughts are just the energy of the universe dancing in your awareness, rising up and falling away again. To debate within yourself whether these ideas are valid or invalid is to become increasingly embedded in them. But such an inner debate is of the same nature as the original ideas: just more thinking. Instead of debating the validity of such ideas, you can learn to relate to them as what they are: just thoughts arising and falling, just mental events coming and going.

There are two important things to understand about nonself: the pain of clinging to self, and why we resist this insight.

The Pain of Clinging to Self

The Buddha realized that we suffer because we believe ourselves to be a separate self, an entity moving unchanged through space and time. Because we see ourselves in this manner, we feel alienated and alone in the vast emptiness of the cosmos. As separate little bits of reality, we have to compete and struggle to wrest what we need from the world. We have to be ourselves, free ourselves, and fix ourselves. What a relief to step outside this imprisoning paradigm!

When we're driving on the freeway, caught in heavy traffic that snails forward an inch at a time, it's overwhelming to think of our separateness. All the people in the traffic with us are separate individuals, each wanting only what he wants, each fighting to make progress at the expense of the others around him. At work, most everyone around us is only a competitor or potential competitor. Even with our friends and family, we have to try to manipulate and maneuver to get what we want. In reality, nonself isn't depressing; what's depressing is all this fighting and struggling and competing as an isolated self, cut off from others and seeking solely one's own advantage.

When we add the notion of self to our experience, we also suffer because of our identification. If someone slanders us, yells at us, or hurts us, thoughts and feelings of anger or sadness arise. That in itself is natural, and not a problem as far as it goes. But it *becomes* a problem when we add, "I am suffering! I am sad! I am angry! And this is awful!" Of course, we prefer pleasant feelings to unpleasant ones, but it's only truly awful that unpleasant feelings

49

are arising within us if we identify with them: this feeling is "mine," or even, this feeling is "me." At that point, we're in trouble.

Further, our notion of self extends beyond the limits of our own organism and its thoughts and sensations. In fact, our identification extends to just about everything around us. It becomes *my* house, *my* clothes, *my* job, *my* car, *my* food, and even *my* spouse or partner, *my* children, *my* parents, and *my* friend. By extending our identification of what is self, we multiply exponentially our opportunities for misery. Every loss or difficulty I encounter with one of the things I see as mine causes me to suffer. It's like having hypersensitive feelers sticking out everywhere from our bodies into the world beyond our skin, causing us great pain at even the slightest touch.

Because of this extended identification of self, we grasp at things. We want the sense of self to extend into everything and everyone. We exhaust ourselves to get more things, and suffer when we lose things—as inevitably, invariably, and ultimately will happen anyway. "Is there anything," asks the Buddha, "that you can hold on to with attachment that will not cause anxiety, exhaustion, sorrow, and despair?"

The paradigm of self perpetuates violence, for seeing some things as self implies seeing other things as not self. And what we see as not self, what we don't identify with, is alien, separate, and suspect. Anything that's not "mine" is threatening, and I can therefore treat it harshly without troubling my conscience. It's because we see people in war as "other," giving them derogatory names, that we can feel okay about hurting, maiming, or killing them and their children, the so-called collateral damage of war. And, of course, since they see us the same way, they are free to do the same to us.

What we see as not us, which we can then kill or injure without worry or guilt, also constantly changes. If my friend does something to make me angry, then he's no longer my friend. Then I can hurt him or, at a minimum, write him off and neglect him.

If my sister says something I don't like, I can say she's no longer my sister. Then I no longer have to relate to her.

We not only have to protect ourselves from our own and others' *misfortune*, but we even have to find a way to protect ourselves from others' *good* fortune. If something good happens to a friend—whether professional success, love, or whatever—and if it's something we also want for ourselves, envy arises. If we identify with that feeling, we suffer. To protect ourselves from such an unpleasant feeling, we engage in psychological defense mechanisms. In the most primitive form, denial, we don't even let ourselves become aware of the simple truth that we feel envious. Alternatively, we might try to minimize the friend's experience in some way. We manage to find a way to see the good that has come to our friend as not really so desirable. We may try to see our friend as lucky rather than deserving. All of this is because we don't know how to simply be happy for the good that comes to others.

When freed from the notion of self, we are also free from grasping. And when we stop grasping and struggling, we cease suffering. We can appreciate the good things that come to others as much as the good things that come to us. We can also learn to be present with equanimity to difficult things. For though there's a deep fear in us that if we let go, we will lose our happiness, the truth is the opposite: the more we let go, the happier we become. To end identification with self is to end our suffering.

Why We Resist No Self

The sense of being a self is deeply embedded in us. It's a very convincing, persistent illusion, one that's difficult to release. We have had the habit of thinking about ourselves as separate since very early in life. But an illusion is an illusion, nonetheless.

Albert Einstein and other theoretical physicists have maintained that time is illusion. Since it was Einstein who said this, we think it must be true. And so we accept it, at least superficially.

But consider: If time is an illusion, what are we? What is a self? If part of what gives me a feeling of being an enduring self is the sense that I extend across time, then what am I if time itself is unreal?

If you take seriously the insight of no self, you may become a little afraid. That fear can cause us to hold on tightly to our sense of self, resisting the Buddha's insight. But the Buddha isn't saying you don't exist, just that you don't exist in the way you normally imagine. You don't lose anything by understanding nonself. You can't lose what's not real.

No self is not a concept but an anticoncept, a kind of medicine the Buddha offers to open us up to a new experience, an experience less closed and claustrophobic, less neurotic and defended, freed from the identification and grasping that cause us to suffer. The Buddha never offered no self as absolute truth, but as what Buddhists call "skillful means," something intended to free us to see in a new way. Clinging to concepts is dangerous, and the Buddha warned that clinging to no self as a concept is even worse than clinging to self.

The fear of letting go of self is deeply programmed into us. It isn't always easy to let go in the face of this fear. It's like clutching an object tightly in your fist, fearing you'll lose everything if it slips from your grasp.

Just learn to gently and patiently unclench your fingers. Don't try to force yourself in a harsh way. Only an open hand can receive.

The Five Aggregates

When the Buddha looked within, he didn't find a self. What he found instead was something he called the five aggregates (*skandhas*), or heaps; in other words, simply a pile of interdependent elements heaped together, cumulatively creating something that appears to be a self. Here are the five aggregates:

- form

- feeling

- perception

- mental formations

- consciousness

Each of these five aggregates is a constantly flowing and changing stream. The teaching of the five aggregates isn't a way to parse reality into rigorously accurate and nonoverlapping pieces, but a way of practicing. Each aggregate can be a subject of meditation, for you to see exactly what's there and realize that none of it constitutes a solid and enduring self.

Form

The aggregate of *form* includes all physiological and physical phenomena. Most important in terms of practice is that form means your body. Mindfulness of the body is called the first foundation of mindfulness. What's happening with your body right now, as you read this? Are there places of tension? What exactly is that tension like? These questions don't require verbal answers, but are invitations to look deeply. When you do this, you are practicing mindfulness of form.

Feeling

The aggregate of *feeling* is about sensation. It includes an awareness of whether the sensation is pleasant, unpleasant, or neutral. When you stub your toe, you can't help but be mindful of the fact that you're having an unpleasant sensation. But you might not always be aware of more subtle feelings, such as your breathing.

When you become aware of your breathing, it may seem neutral at first. And because it seems neutral, trying to focus on it can even create an unpleasant feeling of boredom. But if you attend to your breath mindfully, you can come to experience it as pleasant. Breathing in is like a refreshing glass of cool water on a hot day. You can experience the pleasant release as you breathe out, cleansing and calming body and mind. When you attend to your breath in this way, a neutral experience becomes a pleasant one.

The element that judges our feelings as pleasant, unpleasant, or neutral is known in Buddhist psychology as *manas*. This is where the sense of "I" or ego, the sense of self, creeps in. When we experience pleasant or unpleasant sensations through manas, we're no longer in simple awareness. Something else has been added. Instead of just being aware that "there's an unpleasant feeling here" or "there's a pleasant feeling here," we experience it more like "I'm having a pleasant feeling, and I want this!" or "I'm having an unpleasant feeling, and I want it to go away." But all that's really happening is a feeling is arising along with a judgment about it.

From moment to moment, feelings arise and fall—again and again. And along with them, this process of judging the feeling also comes up. If there's a sense that a feeling is unpleasant, then we automatically assume there must be someone doing the judging. This creates the illusion of something solid that we call an "I," an ego, or a self. It's like how the rapid succession of still photographs in a movie creates the semblance of continuous motion. What really exists is simply the rapid succession of still photos, but the illusion seems quite real to us. In the same way, the rapidly flowing stream of feelings and judgments about the feelings creates the illusion of a self. But what's really there, when we look closely, is just the arising of feelings, one after another, along with our attendant judgments about the feelings.

Perception

The aggregate of *perception* includes recognizing what something is. If we see a cloud, we know it's a cloud. If we see a tree, we know it's a tree. However, this process is faulty in many ways. For one, the real tree is different from our idea of the tree, as we have seen. But also, to use the classic example from the Buddhist sutras, at twilight we might see a piece of rope on the ground and believe it to be a snake, causing fear to arise, even though this fear is based on a faulty perception.

It's surprising how faulty perception can be, as every introductory psychology student knows. We see a circle even though the curved line doesn't close up completely. We see as movement a series of lights that come on sequentially. And our distorted perception is especially important in our relations with other people. Have you ever been startled to realize that someone close to you misperceives you in a fundamental way? This happens all the time, and often we aren't even aware of it. And while we can't always change that person's view of us, we can look into the nature of our own perceptions, realizing that they, too, will be inaccurate quite often. By repeatedly asking ourselves, "Am I sure?" we can gradually come to a deeper and more accurate view.

Mental Formations

The aggregate of *mental formations* concerns our varying psychological states. We have the mental formations of love, peace, happiness, and joy on the one hand, and of jealousy, envy, anger, hatred, and sadness on the other. Some of these are wholesome, meaning conducive to our becoming awake and free. Some are unwholesome, meaning they tend to keep us captive and to lead us in the direction of suffering. Whether a mental formation is wholesome or unwholesome isn't just a matter of whether we experience it as pleasant or unpleasant. If we have a feeling of guilt, for example, this might be a wholesome feeling if it's based on reality rather than neurotic self-doubt. Thus, if I have done something wrong and a guilty feeling arises, that feeling is appropriate. It's wholesome because it teaches me to change my behavior. I don't need to torture myself over it—which adds absolutely nothing. But I can learn the lesson and change.

Consciousness

Consciousness, the fifth aggregate, is the container for our feelings, perceptions, and mental formations. Consciousness has the function of maintaining, cognizing, comparing, storing, and remembering. We know our consciousness primarily through its content rather than in itself.

Nāmarūpa: A Simpler Approach

If this seems complicated, the Buddha sometimes condensed the five aggregates into the simpler term *nāmarūpa*. *Nāma* means "mind," and *rūpa* means "body," so together they mean the mind and body. Whether you work with the five aggregates or with nāmarūpa, these descriptions are all about practice. They are subjects for meditation. You can look into yourself as form, feeling, perception, mental formation, and consciousness, or you can simply look at nāmarūpa. To look into nāmarūpa means to ask, What's my mind like right now? What's my body like right now? In these flowing streams of experience, is there anything stable and solid that's I? This is an important practice of mindfulness.

The Buddha didn't offer the teaching of the five aggregates or of nāmarūpa as the right or only conceptual schema to use to look at what we really are. Other ways can be devised. But the point is, when we break down our experience of what we are in such a way, we can more easily see that there's no self to be found in these elements. Looking into these elements is a way of liberating us from the idea of self, a way to break the illusion. Each is a fluid, dynamic process, not a static and unchanging self.

Deepening Our Understanding of No Self

The belief that we are a separate and unchanging entity called a self is the source of all our misery. Therefore, by removing this delusion, we create the ground for our happiness and well-being. Since this is so crucial, and since the illusion of self is so persistent, let's look into this more deeply.

The point of no self is that, while you do exist, you don't exist in the way you normally imagine. When you say, "I exist," there's the matter of this troublesome little word "I." I, being a noun, seems to refer to something static and solid. But if you look closely, you can see that this isn't what you are at all. You are a living, changing, evolving process. It's not that you're nothing, but that you're not a thing.

To exist means to stand out from the ground of being as something individual and separate. But is that what we really are?

From the viewpoint of the Buddha, nothing is separate. Everything is interconnected. Everything depends on everything else, so much so that we can follow the lead of Zen master Thich Nhat Hanh in saying that nothing is in itself alone, but everything *inter-is* with everything else (1988). You think that you "are," but it's more accurate to say that you "inter-are." You see yourself as something separate from the tree in your yard, but this isn't the case. The tree is creating oxygen for you to breathe in, and you create carbon dioxide for the tree. You may think of yourself as separate from the cloud, but the cloud is water, and you are mostly water. Remove the water element from yourself, and what remains is only a few pounds of minerals, not a living being. What if we remove the sun? Could you exist without the sun? No, you and the sun inter-are. And everything you see is like that. In this way, the existence of one thing in the universe implies the existence of everything else. Some of these relationships are known and apparent, like the water and the sun. Others are subtle and mysterious. But ultimately everything is interconnected and inseparable. One bit implies all the other bits. Removing one bit removes everything.

Sometimes people accept the idea of impermanence but reject the idea of no self. It seems so obvious that we are a self. But impermanence and no self are really the same thing viewed from different angles. Impermanence and no self inter-are. Because we are impermanent, we are not an unchanging self, but a flowing life process that's interconnected and interdependent with everything else. We couldn't really exist without everything else any more than a tree can exist without the earth. While this is very different from our usual way of seeing, it's more accurate. It's also far more interesting than the way we usually see things. When we look with the eyes of no self, everything we see becomes a manifestation of the whole. An ordinary pebble in its wonderful, specific, concrete, and unrepeatable "pebble-ness" is not something separate, but a manifestation of the whole cosmos.

What You Really Are

What are you then?

You are a pattern of energy flowing in the stream of time. Consider a stream of water. In one place, the root of a tree juts out into the stream. The root creates an eddy, an energy pattern in the form of a swirl of water. The particular molecules of water involved in this pattern change continually. And yet there's also continuity. The water continues to swirl in more or less the same way, in much the same pattern, and will continue to do so until the causes and conditions that create the swirl change.

You are just such a patterned flow. There's enough pattern and continuity that people recognize you from day to day, and have the feeling they know who you are and how you're likely to speak and act. But you, too, are changing all the time. Just as the eddy isn't really separate from the river, you aren't separate from the ground of being.

Look at an ordinary table. What's a table? If you remove one of its legs, is it still a table? What if you remove two legs? If the top is made of wood planks running lengthwise, what happens if you remove one plank? Is it still a table? How many planks would you have to remove before it's no longer a table? We treat a table as though it were a kind of self, an inherently existing thing, but when you look more closely, it's very difficult to find the table. If you remove the wood element from the table, then the table ceases to be. If you remove the sunlight element from the table, then there's no tree, and again no table. If you remove the great-grand-mother of the carpenter who made the table, then, again, no table.

If we look with the eyes of a physicist, the table becomes less and less a solid, separate entity. The physicist knows the table is nothing solid at all, but is composed of rapidly moving molecules. The molecules themselves are composed of atoms, and the atoms are composed of subatomic particles. The table is more space than solid matter. And even the solid bits aren't so solid, since even the subatomic particles they are composed of don't exist continuously from moment to moment, but actually pop in and out of existence. Some physicists theorize that when particles pop out of existence in our dimension, they may pop into existence in another dimension. But in any event, our table is far more mysterious and fascinating than we normally suspect.

Consider a wave on the ocean. The wave is also an energy pattern. It arises, continues for a time, and then ceases. But the wave isn't separate from the ocean. The ground of being of the wave is water. Insofar as we think of it as a wave, it appears to be something separate. But it's really the same thing as the water, just manifesting in this way for a time and then ceasing to manifest.

Would it make sense for the wave to say, "I'm better than other waves because I'm larger than they are" or "I'm better, because I'm a more attractive wave than those other waves"? Does it have any meaning for a wave to say to itself, "I'm not as good as other waves"? What if some other waves got together and decided a particular wave wasn't as good as they, and decided to have nothing to do with that wave. Would that make sense? On the other hand, if one wave decided to help another wave, would this be something grand and important? Every wave arises from the ground of its being, the water, and returns to it, making all such comparisons nonsense. And a wave helping another wave won't think it's doing anything special if it knows that both ultimately are water.

The Buddha said we are like fire. The fire also seems to be a separate thing, a self. But looking more closely, we see that the fire changes all the time. It moves this way and that way. A tongue of flame leaps up for a moment and then subsides. The fuel that's the ground of the fire changes from moment to moment as the energy of old fuel is spent and new fuel uncovered. Is it the same fire from moment to moment? It wouldn't be quite accurate to say it's the same, nor could we comfortably say it's different. The fire is really a process.

By way of further example, let's say you are a Yankees fan or a Dodgers fan. What's Yankees? What's Dodgers? As you root for your team over the years, everything about the team changes. The ownership changes. The manager changes. All the players change. The stadium and field change. The uniforms change. Even the rules of baseball aren't eternal verities, but also change from time to time (as with the advent of the designated hitter rule, for example). So when you root for the Yankees or the Dodgers, when you become elated if they win and downcast if they lose, what are you really rooting for?

And yet there's continuity with your team also. Organizations tend to maintain patterns of thinking and operating, even when all the people in the organization have been replaced. The Yankees continue to have a certain ethos of pride and achievement, the Dodgers their ethos of underdogs rising heroically to the occasion. Even though everything is flowing and changing, there's also continuity and pattern. We don't have to deny either the continuity or the change, but we usually underestimate the change while focusing on the continuity. Because we have a word called "team," we imagine something static and stable. But when we look more closely, things aren't as we imagine. This world of change and continuity is a far more interesting and miraculous place than the one we normally inhabit. To be able to see the world of ordinary objects and living beings this way—seeing them as flowing and changing, selfless, and interconnected—is to give rise to what the Buddha called "investigation of phenomena," one of the seven factors of enlightenment.

The French philosopher René Descartes tried to look into the nature of no self but, in the end, had to pull himself back from the brink of the emptiness he discovered. He contemplated a piece of wax, because it softens and changes shape. He noticed that the wax changed and changed again, yet somehow, despite these changes, we think of it as the same piece of wax. We tend to think it's the same piece of wax through all these transformations. A Buddhist might say we have a self-view of the wax. When Descartes went on to ponder whether he himself actually existed, it must have been frightening. Finally he clutched at his famous formula, *cogito ergo sum*, "I think, therefore I am." This must have relieved him greatly. But does it really solve the problem? We may be aware that thinking is occurring, but does that necessarily imply a thinker? No "I" can be established. All we really know is that there's a process going on called thinking.

In fact, we could even say, "I think, therefore I am not." We can get so lost in our thinking that we are not really present, not really alive. Lost in our thinking and ideas, we see the world as spectral and abstract. Only when our frantic thinking calms down can we succeed at being alive, being aware of our breathing, seeing the tree, tasting our coffee.

Sometimes we think the "I" is the one who's watching and observing. But what happens to this observing "I" when we stop observing? For this observing "I" is also something that comes and goes, flickering like the film at the cinema, popping in and out of existence like those subatomic particles. In other words, the observing "I" is nothing substantial either, but is itself a process. It's simply another mental formation, and like all mental formations, it arises in our consciousness, continues for a time, and then ceases.

The Three Traps of Self

In Buddhist teaching, there are three ways in which we can get trapped in the notion of self. The first is the trap of "I" or "me." For example, you might say to yourself, "I am this body." This is a very different way of seeing things from the simpler observation, "There's a body here." When we identify with something in this way, we introduce a lot of suffering. When the body gets sick or ages, we then feel, "I am sick" and "I am growing old."

The second trap is the trap of *object of self*. This occurs when we say to ourselves (staying with the example of the body), "This body is mine." In this way of thinking, rather than see yourself as your body, you see your body as something you possess. Anything we possess introduces the idea of nonpossession, of loss. If we can own it, we can lose it. The same is true when we say *my* job, *my* family, *my* spouse, *my* child, *my* house, or *my* car. In the light of no self, what's a job? What's your husband or your wife? They are flowing processes of change with a semblance of continuity. How can a *process* be "mine"? And who is this "I" that owns this process?

When you look in this way, you see a process of change claiming ownership of another process of change. It can make you laugh out loud.

The third trap of self is called *mutual intercontaining*. In the case of the body, we say, "I am in this body" or "This body is in me." Though more subtle, this is still a form of identification. And whatever we identify with causes sorrow. What we disidentify from brings freedom and joy.

When we let go of self, and see ourselves and everything as simply part of this swirling, living energy that's the universe, everything that troubles us ceases to do so. And there can be joy. There can be peace. There can be happiness.

Escaping Nihilism

It would be easy to get the impression here that the insight of no self is nihilistic, that the Buddha is telling us that nothing is real and nothing really matters. If we take it this way, we can end up in despair: Eat, drink, and be merry, for tomorrow we die. It's all meaningless. But that would be a dangerous misunderstanding. To take it that way is to be bitten by the snake. Clearly, the peace and happiness of the Buddha are not founded on nihilism.

In fact, in the Maharatnakuta Sutra, the Buddha explicitly rejected nihilism. He said, "It is better to be caught in the idea that everything exists [a self point of view] than to be caught in the idea of emptiness [a no-self point of view]. Someone who is caught in the idea that everything exists can still be disentangled, but it is difficult to disentangle someone caught in the idea of emptiness" (Thich Nhat Hanh 1993, 33; bracketed text added).

You won't get caught in nihilism if you remember that the Buddha wasn't trying to replace a faulty dogma with a better one. When he talks about impermanence and no self, he's not suggesting these as better concepts for us to use and cling to. Remember, these insights are anticoncepts. They are designed to break up the distorted lenses through which we see the world. Don't treat the anticoncept as a new concept and carry it on your head like the raft you already used to cross the river. The Buddha is using these insights to help us see in a new way, to help open us to how things really are. The promise is that if we practice with these insights, if we come to look at things this way, we can free ourselves from suffering. We can be liberated and happy people.

The Middle Way

Everything is impermanent, but there's also some continuity. You are not a self, but you still exist. Sometimes it can seem to us that the Buddha is talking out of both sides of his mouth!

The problem, however, is not with the Buddha's teaching. The problem lies with the nature of thinking. We think in discrete Aristotelian categories. Something is this, or it's that. It's one kind of thing or another kind of thing, but not both. A can't be B, and B can't be A. That's how we normally think. That's how we normally imagine the world to be.

The wisdom of the Buddhist tradition is very different. Instead of the boxlike categories of thought, where A is not B, we have the deep insight that A is not A, and that's what makes it truly A. This is not really as difficult to understand as it might seem at first. It means that the flower (A) is not a flower in the way we usually mean, because it's also the sunshine (B). And it's this inter-connection with the sunshine that makes it a flower in the deepest sense of the word, in the light of interbeing. The flower that we see as a separate thing, unrelated to everything else, is illusory. Only the flower that inter-is with everything else is the real flower.

In summer, a tree in my backyard brings forth long, cone-shaped clusters of delicate purple blossoms. The honeybees love those blossoms. They swirl around them in a dance, drunk from the nectar. When you look at the tree and the bees, it's not difficult to see that they are not two things, but one thing. There's a process going on that's really one process. The tree and the bees inter-are.

When we are caught in the view of self, we think of things as either being or not being, as being either a permanent self or on the way to annihilation. The way things really are is somewhere in between being and nonbeing. Things exist, but not in the way we normally think. When we contemplate the way things actually are, saying that things are or are not doesn't quite capture the truth. Nor is it quite true to say that things are permanent, on the one hand, or annihilated, on the other, since the process continues in some form. We will return to this theme in chapter 9, where we take up the subject of death and rebirth.

Reality itself is what the Buddhists refer to as suchness (*tathata*, as introduced in chapter 1)—just so. The Buddha liked to be called the *Tathāgata*, the one who comes and goes in suchness, who lives in the way things really are. Reality is this flowing and changing, living, dynamic process, with everything connected to everything else. Reality is not captured in the conceptual boxes we habitually use. When we see that we are 70 percent or more water, we know that water isn't something separate from ourselves. We are the water. And since we are the water, it's impossible to pollute our streams and oceans with impunity. We can only think that way if we imagine ourselves and the water to be separate things, as though we lived in the hermetically sealed containers of separate selves. Because this isn't so, to pollute the stream is to pollute ourselves.

To see this also means we look at the water differently. When the water is in us, it seems to be part of a living being. Then is it quite accurate to think of the water outside of ourselves as nonliving, as something dead? If water is a living reality inside our bodies, it's also a living reality outside of them. The distinction between living being and nonliving being breaks down.

To see things in their suchness is to see their impermanent and selfless nature, to appreciate the incredible, ungraspable wetness of water, the wonderful rockiness of stone, the springy green leafiness of a leaf. It's also to appreciate that the leaf, the stone, and the water are not separate. Nor is the observer separate.

If you see a flower, you normally think that you, the one doing the seeing, and the flower, the object being seen, are different things. That's how things seem when we view the world through the lens of our concepts. But in reality, where there's seeing, there's always both a seer and something being seen. Seer and seen arise together. It's only in the abstract that these can be separated. In our thoughts and in our language, we separate these things from each other. Our grammar requires a verb to have a subject. That's why we have to say, "It's raining," though "raining" already tells us all we need to know. For this reason, we think there is something called "I" seeing something called "flower." But in suchness, in reality, what we have is something more like "I-seeing-flower"— one inseparable process. When you view the world this way, you begin to know it for the miraculous place it really is.

Since this is so different from the way we normally see things, you might like to dwell on this chapter a while, reading it over slowly to yourself, contemplating key passages without trying to think about it as much as let it soak in, letting these insights penetrate you, letting them become part of you. When the insights in this chapter penetrate you, you will have begun to loosen the grip of your sorrow. You will have become a happier person.

Practice:
Butter in the Sun (No Self)

The inspiration for this practice comes from a Tibetan teacher who promised that it can be a lot of help.

Get into a comfortable position for meditation. If you sit, make sure you are upright, but not rigid, with your head, neck, and back aligned. Sit in a position you can maintain comfortably for some time. You can also try this while lying flat on the floor or on a mat without using a pillow.

Close your eyes and bring your awareness to your breath. When you have established a focus on your breath, imagine yourself to be a slab of butter left out on a window ledge in the warm summer sun. As the light, warmth, and radiance penetrate you, feel yourself melt away. If you are lying down, let yourself melt into the floor. Let all your worries and fears melt into the light and merge with it, losing the sense of the hard edges of self that separate you from the rest of life. Continue for a pleasant length of time.

chapter 3

Releasing Habit Energy

There is nothing worth getting or being.

—Achaan Buddhadasa

You finally get some time to relax, so you stop all that "doing" for a while and sit outside on your patio. There's a feeling of release, and you sigh lightly as you settle into your chair. Finally! You are free. At last you can be happy. Yet within only a few moments, your thoughts begin to drift. Scarcely aware of your thoughts, you find yourself miles away from the chair and the patio and the outdoors. Suddenly, an energy arises in you, and not quite realizing what you're doing, you start sweeping or working in the garden or just tidying up a bit. Before you know it, you've created a little project for yourself, and you're busily "doing" again.

Or perhaps you decide to sit in meditation for a while. You sit on your cushion and find a comfortable posture. You enjoy a few breaths, but all of a sudden, the same pattern emerges. First the mind drifts sideways—into that place where you don't even quite realize it's happening. Suddenly you develop an itch and find yourself scratching. The body starts complaining, and you start wriggling, moving, and adjusting. The more you move, the more you seem to need to move. Then you think of a phone call you have to make. You try to tell yourself you'll remember to make the call after sitting, but you can't get it out of your mind. You try to push the thought away, but it only grows stronger. You tell yourself, "Oh, I'll just place the call and then get right back to this." You make the call. But the call stirs up other thoughts and worries, making you even more restless than before. Your body wriggles and squirms. Finally you give up and do something else—almost anything will do.

When this happens, you have just suffered a close encounter with your habit energy (*vāsāna*). You are being pushed around by it, controlled like a marionette. You may think you're in charge, but you're not: *it* is. Such a habit of restless activity can seem harmless enough, but some habits aren't so innocent. Habits that push us into destructive ways of being and doing are some of the strongest forces aligned against our happiness. Learning to release the energy of these habits transforms them into the energy of happiness.

The Buddha used several powerful images to convey the nature of habit energy. He compared our habit energy to someone being thrown into a pit of burning fire. Two strong men hold her, one on each side. Of course, she is terrified and wants to avoid her fate. But however much she struggles, she can't resist; she's headed for the fire pit.

The Buddha also said habit energy is like a very thirsty person about to drink from a bottle. Suddenly someone warns him to stop, for the water is poisonous. But the thirsty person can hardly help it. His terrible thirst compels him to drink, though he knows it will destroy him.

In a third analogy, the Buddha compared habit energy to what happens when a small bird has stolen a piece of meat and flies up in the air with it. When a larger bird comes to take the meat from the smaller one, the smaller bird can't bring herself to let go. Despite the possibility of being killed by the larger bird, she just can't do it. She can't bring herself to release the precious bit of meat.

In modern psychology, the power of this force is called conditioning. Because of our conditioning, we tend to respond in similar situations the same way we responded in the past. The consequences of our actions, positive or negative, determine how likely we are to do the same thing in the future. We're more likely to repeat actions with pleasing consequences, and less likely to repeat actions with adverse consequences. What's more, short-term consequences exert greater control than long-term consequences. Because of this powerful force, we may know full well that we shouldn't do something because of its negative long-term consequences, but if the immediate consequences are very pleasant, it's hard to resist. Even someone with lactose intolerance can find ice cream hard to resist.

We can get very trapped by our conditioning. When given a shock it can't escape, a laboratory animal placed on an electrified grid clearly displays its distress. It frantically tries to do something to escape the shock. But once it learns that nothing it does results in relief, the animal gives up. After this, even when the experimenter changes the conditions of the experiment so that only half the gird is electrified and half isn't, the animal may never learn that it can escape the shock by simply moving to the other part of the grid. It has learned to be helpless in the face of the shock and no longer seeks a solution. It no longer even tries to find an answer.

Our habit energy is so strong. Though sometimes we may be able to assert our freedom and make a conscious choice, sometimes our habit energy pushes us around ruthlessly and irresistibly. Habit energy can be much stronger than our intention to change, making us feel helpless. It seems as if we can do nothing but continue in our destructive, unhappy patterns.

If we appreciate the power of the force of conditioning, we won't treat ourselves harshly. Doing so only adds more flames to the fire pit, more insatiability to our thirst, more of a tendency to cling in spite of the danger. Instead, if we clearly see the powerful grip of these factors, we can learn to allow compassion to rise within us, both for ourselves and for others who are caught in their own conditioning. Happiness arises out of kindness, not struggle or harshness.

New Year's Resolutions

Sometimes we use the occasion of New Year's Day to prod ourselves to change. We will exercise, eat more healthfully, lose weight, stop smoking, and so on. We may stick with it for a while, but at some point, within a few days or weeks, the all but inevitable occurs. We go back to our old ways.

This vicious cycle can happen not only on an annual but also on a seasonal or even a daily basis. Someone tells herself in April, "I have to lose weight before swimsuit season arrives," but once again finds this difficult to do. Or someone tells himself every morning, "Today I'm going to the gym after work," but finds that as the stresses of the day wear on him, he can hardly help himself. Once again he finds himself sitting in front of the television rather than working out.

We get caught in perfectionistic and absolutist approaches. We impose rules on ourselves, such as "I will exercise every day." But once we violate the rule, we feel helpless. We become like the animal on the electrified grid. Seeing no way to change, we give up altogether.

In the psychology of addictive behavior, giving up after failing to adhere to an absolute rule is a well-known phenomenon called the *abstinence violation effect*. It concerns an addicted person's tendency to give up after even a single violation of the rule of total abstinence. This is why the alcoholic who slips up once tells herself, "It's hopeless. I'll never be able to change." She gives up. When the next drink is offered, she tells herself, "Oh what the heck, I've already blown it anyway," and goes on drinking.

Black-and-white thinking and perfectionism undermine our efforts to change. If the habit energy is weak, we may simply have the insight that a certain behavior isn't conducive to our well-being, and then just change it. But if the habit energy is strong, we must somehow persist in trying to change, even in the face of setbacks and backsliding, without trivializing them but also without permitting them to become an invitation to hopelessness or despair. Hopelessness and despair are not only very painful, but also excuse us from further effort. If we think the situation is hopeless, then we're justified in not trying.

Generally, it's better to understand that change is a matter of patience and persistence, setbacks and renewed effort, rather than sudden perfection. Change is a process of making mistakes, and then learning from our mistakes and trying again. Since you are a process, not a separate self, it isn't surprising that changing your habit energy is also a process. It's better for us to walk in the right direction than to enforce a rigid perfectionism.

Bringing Mindfulness to Habit Energy

When our conditioning compels us to knowingly act in ways that are contrary to our well-being, when the habit is too strong and we can't just simply bring ourselves to change, we are in a key place to practice nonstruggle. At this point, you realize you've tried pushing yourself already, and it hasn't worked. In fact, you've seen that the more you struggle, the worse the situation becomes. Struggling creates more tension in us, which then becomes a reason to persist with the unwanted behavior. While we persist in the belief that struggle leads to happiness, struggle is self-perpetuating: it can only create more struggle. Struggle lures us farther and farther away from well-being.

Fortunately, there's another way. There's a way between helplessness on the one hand, and struggle on the other. Instead of struggling, we can learn to bring mindfulness to our habit energy. Become aware, in an accepting way, of just what's going on. See it clearly and kindly. What are the external cues that trigger the unwanted behavior? What sort of internal cues—thoughts and emotions—continue to pull you in that direction? Where do you feel the pull of habit energy in your body, and exactly what is that sensation like? If you indulge habit energy, what happens? What do you experience? What happens now, and what happens later? Trace cause and effect. Become aware of your breathing, and watch all of this with calmness, clarity, and serenity. Positive change doesn't grow from a confused, irritated, conflicted mind, but out of your mindfulness. Keep nourishing the energy of mindfulness in you, and what seems impossible now, you will one day be able to do.

The Habit of Overusing Substances

Overusing drugs, alcohol, or cigarettes is the most destructive habit we have to deal with. It's no wonder the Buddha taught to refrain from using intoxicants as one of the five basic precepts. Today, however, we face even more addictive substances. As far as we know, nothing existed in the Buddha's time with the addictive potential of cocaine or methamphetamine. These substances are so addictive, laboratory animals work themselves to death to receive a dose of them.

Rebecca came to me for help changing her drinking habit. She had already tried AA and found it wasn't for her. At first, we dealt with this in a straightforward manner. We approached her difficulty in accord with the best approaches known to modern research. I assessed her degree of preparedness to change. I intervened to enhance her motivation. We talked about skills and strategies for change. Nothing seemed to help. She kept right on drinking.

Sometimes she found it within herself to stop or reduce her drinking for a while, but then quickly returned to her prior level. We analyzed the chains of behavior that led to drinking. We analyzed how she managed to return to the same pattern, what events and triggers took her back to the same level of drinking. She kept right on with little or no change.

Fortunately, many people change their addictive behavior more easily than Rebecca. Most people do it on their own, without any outside help. But every therapist who works with people suffering from addiction knows clients like Rebecca. Those strong arms kept throwing her into the fire pit.

Gradually, Rebecca and I simply began to relax with the problem. We stepped back from it, stopped struggling. From time to time it resurfaced, and we focused on it when she wanted to. But I didn't insist. We brought mindfulness to whatever came up in session. We talked about other difficulties in her life. We talked about her childhood. We explored her dreams to see what they revealed about her inner life. Gradually, together we reached a deeper understanding of the wounds and vulnerabilities connected to her drinking. Ever so slowly, with many ups and downs, our relationship deepened, and her drinking habit improved.

It was only when we stopped the frontal assault on her drinking—even the very subtle and skillful approaches available to present-day therapists—and learned how to be together in a mindful, healing relationship that the real healing began for Rebecca. Over time, she came to trust that I wasn't judging her or pressuring her to change. At the end of our work together, she still drank, but much less. Only rarely did she overdo it, and when she did, she didn't drive or engage in dangerous activities. The harm alcohol had caused in her life diminished greatly. The way forward meant learning to stop fighting so hard, to stop struggling against her powerful conditioning, and learning to enjoy the positive elements in her life. It meant coming to see herself with kindness.

The Habit of Overeating

Americans are becoming increasingly obese at a younger and younger age. This may be the result of many things, including not having the skills to handle our emotions. While we engage in a lot of self-blame about being overweight, there are actually many contributing factors, including environmental and genetic ones. To say that we are to blame is simplistic. We have bodies that are designed to survive famine by building up stores of fat, while we live in an environment where food is cheap and easily available. Our social lives revolve around food and drink, rather than more active pursuits, so that whenever we get together with other people, we are at risk of gaining more weight. Overweight individuals crave food the way a dehydrated person craves water. It's a powerful drive.

Our sense of satiety lags behind our consumption. Since it takes some time for our feelings of fullness to register, it doesn't help that we eliminate factors that would otherwise slow us down when we eat. Often we don't have to shell our nuts, cut our meat, or make much effort at all. We eat our food on the go, with one hand and little effort or attention. The food industry continually studies how to make appealing products that go down easily. They intentionally stimulate our cravings so we'll eat more of their products. They're not evil for doing this; they're simply trying to make a profit. But in the course of doing so, they create extremely addictive foods, loaded with salt, sugar, and fat. These ingredients, however, only stimulate more cravings. The more of them we eat, the more we want to eat. As we eat more of these foods, our mental circuitry more and more deeply entrenches the habit energy of our craving (Kessler 2009).

Diets only make the problem worse. We lose weight temporarily, and then gain it all back, plus a bit more. A diet is a temporary measure, but what we need is an altered way of living and a different sort of awareness about food. We need a new way of thinking about these matters.

It won't help to castigate yourself if you struggle in this area. It's a difficult thing to change. The deck is stacked against you, making the odds extremely high that you'll continue to gain weight. You *can* lose weight, but it's a process. You have to practice a different kind of intention, persist gently through cycles of failure and success, and transform your habit energy into something more constructive. Often we have to let go of any idea of being perfectly slim—which often boomerangs on us—and focus on losing a bit and being healthy.

If you are one of the few who can see the difficulty, make a plan, and stick with it for life, that's wonderful. But for most, it isn't like that. Most struggle, gaining and losing again and again, or, even worse, give up altogether.

Mindfulness can help. We can learn to eat more slowly and mindfully, aware of each bite of food, each sip of drink. Through mindfulness, we can actually come to enjoy our food more, rather than feel as though we have to sacrifice all pleasure from food. We can also bring awareness to the stresses that compel this difficult habit.

—— Practice: ——
Apple Meditation

To practice eating mindfully, try this meditation. Choose a time when you won't be rushed. Take an apple that's appealing and delicious, or another kind of fruit you enjoy. Cut it into slices. Sit quietly for a few moments, following your breathing and contemplating the apple. Take your time. See the apple in a no-self way; that is, see the sunlight, the earth, the water in the apple. Be aware of all the beings who helped bring it to your table.

Enjoying your movements, slowly bring the apple to your mouth. Notice everything. Do you begin to salivate as you bring the apple toward your mouth? What does the apple smell like? Let your mouth, tongue, lips, and teeth work as they normally would, only perhaps a little more slowly than usual. Notice how the flavor and texture change as you chew the apple. Chew it well, without rushing. When it feels right, let yourself swallow. Note that somehow you just know when it's time to swallow. Notice the process of swallowing. See if you feel the apple go down to your stomach.

Before taking another bite, stop and breathe. Again, look deeply at the apple. Avoid bringing another slice up to your mouth before you have swallowed. You can easily spend fifteen minutes or more just enjoying an apple, noticing everything that occurs during the process of eating. If you do this in a mindful, slow, and enjoyable way, you will never again eat an apple the way you did before.

Once you have been able to enjoy eating an apple in mindfulness, you may be ready to try eating a whole meal mindfully. Contemplate the food before you start to eat. Chew thoroughly, taking your time and eating in a relaxed way. Pause and breathe from time to time. Check in with yourself about how full you feel as you continue to eat. When do you reach the point of being just full enough, satisfied but not stuffed? See if you can stop eating at that point or maybe even just before reaching that point. Or does your habit energy push you around, causing you to keep eating? If it does, just notice. Notice how the habit energy pushes you to continue. Be present to it and mindful, without struggling. Just notice. Just recognize. See exactly how you experience this process in your body and in your thoughts and emotions.

When you can eat a meal this way, move in the direction of being mindful in all your eating and drinking. Be aware of every bite, every sip. Enjoy it deeply and fully, taking your time, just as you did with the apple. Practice in the spirit of nonpractice, of happiness, serenity, and calm. You don't have to eat on the go. You have the right to enjoy a meal without multitasking. At this point, eating and drinking aren't just passing pleasures, or even just ways to nourish the body. They are opportunities for meditation, for mindfulness. They are invitations to practice happiness.

You might enjoy expanding the idea of mindful consumption to include not only literal consumption, but also any kind of sensory experience you take into yourself. You can learn to practice mindful shopping by taking your time and considering each item. Is it necessary? Is it healthy? Sometimes your habit energy causes you to buy things that you don't really need or that aren't healthy for you or for the earth. When this happens, change if you can, but if you can't yet do so, just notice all this. Remaining mindful will build your capacity to make wise choices. You can do the same with your reading material or what you watch on television, in theaters, or on the computer. Learn to be mindful of these forms of consumption as well. Notice how they affect your body and mind. Don't force yourself to give things up. Just be aware, and let mindfulness be the teacher.

Mindfulness is the Buddha's gentle voice within you, teaching you to leave suffering behind and arrive in the Buddha's land of happiness and well-being.

The Habit of Doing

One of our more pervasive habits is the habit of doing rather than being. Even when we have time to relax, we try to *do* our relaxation, engaging in more activities that only leave us more exhausted afterward than we were to begin with. The French philosopher Blaise Pascal said that all of our difficulties come from being unable to sit alone in a room. I call this the "primal itch." It is a restless energy in us that, operating unnoticed, can be a merciless tyrant. The tyranny of doing robs us of our happiness and well-being.

We get very uncomfortable at the prospect of doing nothing. It's as if we are so afraid of being lazy that we must always justify our existence by doing and accomplishing.

Practice:
Nondoing

This practice is designed to help you observe the habit energy of doing, and increase your capacity to just be.

Set a timer for five to ten minutes. Sit on a meditation cushion or chair in an upright but comfortable position. Let your hands rest in your lap or in whatever way is natural for you. Follow your breathing. As you breathe in, say "in" silently to yourself, and as you breathe out, say "out." Resolve to remain still until the timer sounds.

When an impulse to move arises, see about not giving in to it. Notice what this impulse feels like. Notice what the energy in your body is like. Ask yourself if it's okay to be present with this impulse without moving for a while. If you absolutely need to move, do so slowly and mindfully, remaining aware of the intention to move, the feelings in your body, and the exact nature of the movement you make. Notice the result of the movement. Did it bring relief? Or did it stimulate more desire to move?

The first thing you may notice is that this is not as easy as it sounds. For one thing, thoughts come in and pull you away from awareness of breathing. And once you lose the connecting thread of the breath, you may forget your resolve to remain still. You may suddenly find yourself moving, scratching, or adjusting your posture, or you may even find yourself up and doing something before you are quite aware of it.

Please be kind to yourself about this. It's perfectly normal. Ours is a culture of distraction. Many forces have created this strong habit energy in us. Doing this practice gives you the opportunity to observe more closely. If you were able to observe this restless energy with a little more clarity, then you are already successful. Bringing an accepting awareness to your habit energy already puts you on the road to relaxing fully, without restlessness always intruding.

Conditioned to Do

From psychology we know that when we are in a given situation, we tend to do whatever we did in the past. So if every time you sit on your patio to relax, you bounce up quickly to do something that needs to get done, you will strengthen the tendency to do. Whenever you sit there, the itch to do something will continue to arise, and with increasing intensity. If you want to be able to sit and relax, you have to practice not doing sometimes. Then you have both the option of not doing and the option of doing. You have freedom. You have a choice.

When you are working, see if you can catch yourself in the moments between tasks and, without immediately plunging into the next thing to do, pause. Take a few mindful breaths. Be aware of the energy that pushes you relentlessly to do the next thing.

Notice precisely what your thinking is like, what emotions are present, and what your bodily sensations are like. Don't go to war against these impulses; that will only increase the difficulty. Just notice. Slow the impulse down just a bit. And in this way, you will begin to open up a zone of freedom.

The Habit of Craving

Buddhist teaching includes the four "cravings" (*taṇhā*, meaning "craving" or "thirst") for money, sex, power, and fame. When people become Buddhist monks or nuns, they vow to no longer seek these things. Far from being a joyless act of renunciation, when properly approached and understood, this can be an act of joy and freedom.

Those of us who are not monks or nuns need to have some money, may want to enjoy the sexual aspect of our lives, and may not mind having influence and being well-known. But the inordinate pursuit of these things is destructive for us as well. The kind of thinking that says, "I will sacrifice today, pushing myself past my limits and working very hard to make a lot of money, and then tomorrow I will enjoy myself," lacks wisdom. Tomorrow is always uncertain. We need to make today a happy day, whatever our responsibilities may be, and not sacrifice it on the altar of a future that may never arrive anyway.

Craving differs from ordinary wanting. If you are thirsty, you drink water, refreshing yourself and supplying your body with what it needs—no problem there. But craving is different. To crave is to want something that doesn't satisfy us or nourish us. Giving in to a craving is drinking saltwater to quench our thirst. The saltwater doesn't satisfy, and only leaves us wanting more.

Craving is out of proportion with the satisfaction it can actually bring. Happiness can come to us in countless ways, but if we're caught in craving, we're trapped. We think we can only find happiness through the craved object. So we miss the other sources of happiness that are available, and we're ultimately disappointed even if we get what we crave.

A strong connection exists between the energy of craving and that of doing. There's a connection between craving and the primal itch. The habit energy that arises and pushes you to pull up a weed when you intended to sit outside might be rooted in a craving for perfection—in this case, a perfect lawn. Of course, if this is what you want to do, that may be all right. You can mindfully choose to get up and pull the weed. You can pull the weed and then follow through with your intention of enjoying sitting quietly on your porch. But you will have a tendency to go in another direction if mindfulness isn't present. If mindfulness isn't present, after pulling up one weed, you may see another and be compelled to pull it up too, and then another. You're caught in craving. And the next thing you know, you have sacrificed being for doing.

Perhaps this way, you will have a very nice lawn or garden. But when will you be able to stop and enjoy it?

The Spirituality of Getting

In some current forms of spirituality, people focus on manifesting things they want in their lives. If they want more money, a better job, or a loving partner, they focus on bringing these things into their lives.

The Buddha would find this to be a dangerous practice. It may work, but it can easily ensnare us in the realm of ego, of destructive cycles of wanting and getting, and then wanting more. Such practices can focus us too much on what's lacking, instead of helping us be happy in the here and now by being aware of what's already good in our lives. If you use this kind of approach, be mindful about it. Keep it in proportion. Check to see whether it really helps or only stimulates more craving in you. Give gratitude more weight than craving. Make sure it isn't an invitation to disappointment and despair.

Mindfulness Is the Key

Mindfulness is fundamental to change. A lot of our unwanted habits occur when we are unaware. Take, for example, a person who wants to quit smoking. When the phone rings, she answers it and talks with her friend, but then suddenly realizes she has a lit cigarette in her hand. When we bring mindfulness to this situation, it already begins to change. You don't have to go to war with yourself. Just let your mindfulness embrace what's going on. And one day you will be able to change.

Someone once told me that as she continued to practice mindfulness, she discovered one day that she had lost all desire to eat meat. The desire just left her. She didn't struggle over this decision, or have a hard time implementing it or sticking with her intention to change. The decision just arose naturally for her as the fruit of her practice of living mindfully. I don't mean to imply that vegetarianism is the right choice for everyone but, rather, to point out that desires sometimes change easily when we are mindful instead of running on autopilot.

Similarly, another person told me that one day, while talking on the phone with his difficult, angry father, he suddenly found he could remain calm and loving. He wasn't struggling to make this change happen; the capacity suddenly appeared in him. It was the fruit of his mindfulness. He knew that only a few weeks before, he couldn't have done that. But now he could do it almost effortlessly.

While we can train our consciousness, it's always important to do this with kindness and gentleness, not expecting ourselves to do what we're not ready to do. We don't force. We practice with the understanding that happiness is the way, not with a sense that we have to struggle against our habit energies.

Tools for Working with Habit Energy

Nothing typifies the struggle with habit energy as much as drug or alcohol addiction. These habits are really an example of drinking saltwater to quench our thirst. They don't satisfy, but only leave us wanting more. Even if you are dealing with less serious habit energies you wish to change, you can learn from some of the approaches used in addiction treatment. They are another way to bring mindfulness to these difficulties.

——— Practice: ———
Reviewing Your Reasons to Quit

We may have good reasons to quit an unwholesome behavior, but when habit energy strikes, we forget all about them. Our intention to change is in one mental compartment, while the habit energy to continue is in a totally separate one.

There's a simple and direct way to bring these compartments together. When you consider the habit you wish to change, sit down, breathe in and out, and contemplate all the reasons you want to change. Make just one resolution: when the habit energy strikes, you will thoughtfully read over your list before giving in to the behavior. This opens a line of communication between these two mental compartments.

For example, if you want to quit smoking, list the obvious health concerns like lung cancer and all the consequences that could follow from that, such as possibly not living long enough to see your children or grandchildren grow up. But also include reasons that objectively seem inconsequential but may be important to you nonetheless. One individual quit smoking not because of lung cancer but because she didn't like tobacco stains on her teeth and fingers. Call it vanity if you will, but if it works, use it.

As with any practice, you can do this one in either a deep or a superficial way. To do it deeply, breathe in and out, and contemplate each item. Clearly envision the unwanted consequences of indulging the urge. Envision the desirable consequences of not giving in. From time to time, return to your list and add to it. Include as many items as you can. Don't do it like a homework exercise you just want to be done with.

Practice:
Delaying

With some kinds of cravings, just try putting them off until later. If you are concerned about the amount of television you watch in the evenings, and want to modify it rather than give it up altogether, delaying can be very helpful. Instead of starting to watch as soon as you get home from work, you might wait until eight or nine o'clock. This can be a lot easier to do than forcing yourself to quit completely. It avoids the feeling of deprivation that only strengthens our unwanted urges.

When an urge arises to engage in an unhealthy behavior, stop and notice what you're thinking and feeling. Habit energy is like everything else we experience: it comes up in our bodies and our awareness, remains a while, and then subsides again. The actual amount of time the habit energy is powerful and compelling is brief, maybe fifteen to twenty minutes. It helps to remember that the difficult period is so temporary, so impermanent. Instead of fighting the habit energy, you can hold it mindfully, letting yourself know exactly what you're experiencing in your body and mind, and watching as these thoughts, emotions, and bodily sensations change. You can do this safely if you remember that the habit energy is time limited. It will come and go on its own. If you can be present to the habit energy, you don't have to let it push you around. What you can't even let yourself experience becomes more and more frightening. But remaining present to it shows you that there's nothing much to fear. You don't have to deny that the urge is there. You can be like the person on the porch who is aware of the push to attack the weed, but instead decides to continue relaxing, aware of the habit energy arising and passing away.

—— Practice: ——
Taking Time Off

In alcohol treatment, sometimes a therapist asks clients who are unwilling to abstain permanently to consider taking some time off from drinking so they can experience the benefits of sobriety. In addiction treatment, this approach is called *sobriety sampling*. But anyone who's trying to change a behavior can do the same thing by just taking a little time off from the habit. In this way, people can experience a new way of being, without having to fear that the change must be permanent.

You can apply this strategy to any habit that concerns you. If you want to stop snacking in the evenings, resolve to take a break from snacking for a specific period, perhaps a few weeks, just to experience what that's like. If you want to stop using so much sarcasm or cynicism in your speech, try it for a limited time. In this way, you break up the force of the habit and allow yourself to experience the positive consequences of the desired change.

Practice:
Finding an Alternative

To give up something is only half the battle. To do so effectively, you also have to have an alternative. You have to do something else.

If you want to give up alcohol, find a healthy beverage you will allow yourself to enjoy instead. If you want to give up watching television, find something to do in the evening that appeals to you. Finding an alternative helps us to avoid feeling deprived. If we feel deprived about a behavioral change we're trying to make, we won't succeed.

More broadly, finding an alternative is about being able to envision a different way of being. Can you imagine a peaceful, happy evening without television? Can you imagine a happy evening without alcohol or whatever you want to change? Can you imagine modifying your habit energy of excessive "doing"? If you can envision making this change without feeling deprived, you increase your chance of success.

Mind Is Not the Boss

Sometimes we try to approach change only from the rational mind. We set up the rational mind as the boss and put it in charge. But putting the rational mind in charge creates a lot of struggle in us. A lot of who we are isn't rational and reasonable, and those parts of us resist being dominated. The rational part is so small that trying to change through reason alone is like trying to melt a frozen lake with the heat of your finger. Your finger will freeze long before the lake melts.

Mind isn't the boss. Mind is only a part of what we are. When we practice mindfulness, we just let our mind come along for the ride, bringing awareness to each thing we do, feel, and experience. In this way, awareness works in harmony with the rest of what we are. Awareness illuminates each experience, without setting us up to fight. When we try to boss ourselves around, we generate resistance. But if we patiently continue to bring mindfulness to our difficulties, we open the door to change.

Through mindfulness, we may come to see that the things we want so urgently aren't really that important. Once you get them, you clearly see that they aren't such a big deal. When we finally get that long-desired new sports car, we experience pleasure. But how long does it last? Eventually, the new car becomes just part of the backdrop of life as usual. We still have the same commute, the same struggle with traffic. If we're crawling along in the traffic jam at five miles per hour, it matters little whether we are in a new BMW or a clunky old Chevy.

As we bring mindfulness again and again to these kinds of experiences, we learn the truth about our cravings, and it becomes natural for us to live more simply. Rather than being a matter of giving something up, it's more about letting things fall away. The light of the living truth of your own mindfulness illumines the way.

Practice:
Touching the Buddha Within

One way to deal nonviolently with our habit energy is to focus on raising a different kind of energy in us. Then the positive energy takes care of the negative energy.

We all have Buddha nature. This isn't just an expression. Your mindfulness is the Buddha within you. You can get in touch with the Buddha within you at any time, and nourish that kind of energy.

When habit energy strikes, when it starts to push us around, we can stop and breathe. Bring up the image of a peaceful, kind, wise Buddha. Or if you like, bring up the image of someone from your own tradition that represents serenity and wisdom: Christ, a saint, or a wise healer. Imagine what it would feel like to be such a person. Take your time. As you imagine this, you come to experience it too. You come to experience the Buddha within.

To begin, sit and enjoy your breathing, silently saying to yourself "in" on each inbreath and "out" on each outbreath. Then bring up the image of a peaceful Buddha. Breathe in and out with these thoughts, dwelling on each as long as you like:

- I touch the *Buddha within* myself.

- Touching Buddha, I feel *peace*.

- Touching Buddha, I feel *serene*.

- Touching Buddha, I sense the *wisdom* in myself.

- Touching Buddha, I sense the *kindness* in myself.

- Touching Buddha, I nourish my *solidity*.

- Touching Buddha, *I am free*.

After you breathe in and out with each phrase a few times, you can simplify it to just the emphasized words. After a while, if your mind grows quiet, you can even just sit in silence with the intention still wordlessly present. When your focus grows unclear, when you are drifting sideways again, return to the full phrase, then to the emphasized portion, and finally to silence.

After doing this, check in with yourself. How are things with your habit energy? However they are, let them be. Give yourself credit for practicing, not for the immediate result.

Mindfulness Is Being at Peace with Ourselves

When we practice living mindfully and happily, we don't create an inner war. We know how to take care of our habit energy. Fighting against our habit energy only feeds the very tendencies we want to reduce. By embracing these energies, by being willing to experience them with a friendly curiosity, and by nourishing positive energies in our consciousness, we treat ourselves in a kind and nonviolent way. And treating ourselves in a kind and nonviolent way is the essence of mindfulness, the essence of happiness.

In the next chapter, you will learn how to take care of thoughts and feelings with kindness and nonviolence.

chapter 4

Transforming Thoughts and Feelings

It is not things themselves that trouble us, but our thoughts about those things.

—Epictetus

Near the village of Taos, New Mexico, a bridge spans a beautiful and dramatic gorge. You can see how the river water has cut through the rock over the slow centuries, creating the stunning landscape below. A walk over the bridge offers a breathtaking view, inspiring feelings of awe.

But some people have very different feelings on that bridge. Every year, several people commit suicide there, leaping off into the gorge far below. For distraught people who want to make a dramatic end to their misery, the gorge has the same pull as bridges like the Golden Gate in San Francisco and tall buildings like the Empire State Building in New York. As has been done elsewhere, the people of Taos are currently considering whether to create some kind of barrier to prevent these desperate acts.

One plan is to install a safety net, which might be a good idea. But there's another kind of safety net we need, and we need it desperately. We need a net of wisdom. We need the capacity to take care of our emotions. An emotion is not something anyone should ever die over. Like everything else, emotions are marked with impermanence and selflessness. Yet for all our success as a society in other areas, we don't do well at caring for our feelings. Our school curricula don't typically provide information about taking care of this aspect of life. Somehow we're just supposed to know how to do this.

Fortunately, it's something you can learn. In the Buddhist path, mindfulness is the key to the art of emotional self-care. Lately psychology has also been discovering the capacity of mindfulness to change our moods and emotions. It's a powerful approach.

In this chapter, we will examine the nature of our thoughts and feelings, and learn how to transform them.

We Create Our World

Each of us operates out of a worldview that has been shaped by many factors: genetics, childhood experiences, subtle cues about the world we unquestioningly took in from parents and teachers, the events of our personal histories and of collective history. From the flames of these experiences, we forge expectations about life, expectations about relationships, work, what we should feel, and how we should handle those feelings. These expectations differ widely from one person to the next.

Happy people live in a world where good things occur all the time. Loving people see kindness everywhere. Curious people find life endlessly interesting. But unfortunately, angry people inhabit a world of constant injustice. Envious people live in a world where everyone else has more than they do. Sad people are always encountering dispiriting events. Anxious people live in a frightening, unsafe world. How can this be? Don't we all live in the same world?

It works this way because our views of the world are self-perpetuating. Seek and you will find, we read in the New Testament. And we can add, *what* you seek is exactly what you will find. Angry people *focus* on perceived injustice. And since they focus on this aspect of their experience, they find it everywhere. What's more, their anger makes the people around them angry in return, triggering negative reactions from them. Such reactions create further experiences of injustice, confirming the angry person's worldview and providing even more reason to be angry.

There are many variants on this theme. One form is the person who considers herself a good judge of character, without realizing that this focus *causes* her to find everyone's character flaws (except her own). Such a person lives in a world where everyone is deeply flawed and constantly disappoints her, leaving her angry a great deal of the time. Another such person might be so afraid of being taken advantage of that he continually scans for this, and then continually finds it happening. Everyone is out to cheat him.

Only when angry people learn to shift perspective can the pleasantness of life shine forth. If they learn to focus on the kindness that's present in others, the world starts to look less hostile and unfair. If they focus on the good in others, people seem more reasonable. If they focus on the needs and suffering of others, they discover their own compassion and kindness, and come to recognize these qualities in others.

Envious people seldom notice those who have less. Only if they learn to focus on what they already have, only if they can start to see how many people have less, can they transform the bitterness of envy and begin to live in a world of abundance.

The world you experience is the creation of not just sensory experience but also your attitudes, beliefs, and expectations. The world you live in is the product of your mind. You can catch a glimpse of this by simply becoming mindful of how different the world looks to you when you're in different moods. When you're happy, the rain seems soft and friendly, fertile and encouraging. When you're sad, it seems as if the rainy world is, always was, and always will be gray, damp, cold, and uninviting. When you're feeling kind and happy, other drivers on the road seem agreeable and cooperative. You notice the kindness people show in slowing for other drivers to merge ahead of them, in using their turn signals, and in letting others' mistakes go by. When you're angry or sad, the other drivers on the road are all jerks.

We are what we think. This is far more profoundly and extensively true than we imagine. For this reason, the most important thing we need to do to be happy is to heal our minds. When we heal our minds, we can change the situation we're in. Mind and situation are ultimately the same thing, one and inseparable.

Our Sixth Sense

In Buddhism, there are six senses. The sixth sense is nothing supernatural, but simply our own mind. In addition to the hearing, seeing, smelling, tasting, and feeling body, there is the thinking mind, our sixth sense.

This is a unique way to view mental processes. When you really look into what's going on when you think, are you really *doing* something called thinking, or is it simply the case that thoughts arise in your awareness? True, we can "think" in the sense of directing our consciousness toward a certain matter of interest, perhaps a problem we want to solve or a question we'd like to answer. But even then, do we think in the sense of causing thoughts to arise, or do they arise on their own?

Consider what happens with the sense of sight. Do we actually "see," or does seeing simply arise when our eyes make contact with light, resulting in an electrochemical signal to the visual cortex? Again, we can *look* at something, meaning we direct our attention toward a certain visual input, but do we actually do something called seeing, or does seeing simply happen? It's likewise with hearing. We can *listen* in the sense of directing our attention toward certain sounds, but do we actually do the hearing, or does hearing simply arise?

When you look at your actual experience closely, you can readily see that, from a certain point of view, these phenomena *arise*. They are organic phenomena that come up, hang around for a time, and then subside. They are selfless and impermanent. They don't last. There's no one doing something called seeing or hearing or thinking. There are just sights and sounds and thoughts that arise. There's no one doing it, and there's nothing being done. From a certain point of view, they just happen.

This has surprising implications. It means that whenever certain conditions are present, thoughts arise. It would be useless to attempt to prevent this from happening. You can't actually stop yourself from thinking any more than you can stop yourself from seeing when light strikes your retina and the signal is communicated to your brain. Thinking just *happens*. Thoughts just arise. You can work with these phenomena, as I will show you, but to try to avoid having thoughts is useless or worse than useless. It's expending a lot of energy trying to do something that can't be done, like someone who frowns, squints, and strains to try to transport himself instantly to China. The truth is, rivers flow, rain falls, trees leaf, brains think. No matter how you try to avoid it, these things will continue.

When we worry, well-intentioned people tell us, "Just put it out of your mind. Just don't think of it." But since thoughts arise automatically, you won't be very successful at not thinking about something. In fact, what may well happen is that, when you try to keep from thinking, thoughts will still arise, but then you will have added something else: the attempt to avoid knowing they're arising. Doing this launches you into a state of tension and futile struggle, for regardless of whether or not you allow yourself to acknowledge thoughts, they arise. You've succeeded only at turning your consciousness into a battleground.

A Thought Experiment

You can check this out for yourself by trying this thought experiment. After you read this paragraph, close your eyes. And when your eyes are closed, follow this one instruction with all your might. Are you ready? Here it is:

Don't think about flying pigs.

After thirty seconds or so, stop the experiment and open your eyes. Go ahead. I'll wait.

One of two things happened. Most people immediately find that all they can think about is flying pigs. What a strange thing! I'm willing to bet that you don't often go around thinking about flying pigs, but all you have to do to have flying pigs flood your awareness is tell yourself *not* to think about them.

Some have a different experience. They report that, indeed, they were successful: they didn't think about flying pigs at all. This is just a little subtler. But if you fall into this category, ask yourself a simple question: How did you know you weren't thinking about flying pigs? The only way you could do this would be to have the thought "flying pigs" in there somewhere to begin with. You were successful because part of you used the idea of flying pigs to check on whether or not they were present in your awareness. You can only know you're not thinking about something by referring to the very thing you're trying not to think about! In other words, it's in there somewhere regardless. To succeed is to fail.

We don't need to feel discouraged by this failure. It's just how our consciousness works. We have to learn to work with it, instead of trying to do futile things like not think.

Problems Caused by Avoiding Thoughts

Many psychological problems are caused by trying not to think, by trying to avoid certain kinds of inner states. Trying to avoid unpleasant thoughts and feelings can distort our lives and our consciousness.

What if you found that you were only comfortable in your own home, that you felt anxious everywhere else to the point of sometimes even having panic attacks? At first, you might notice a lot of anxiety whenever you travel by air. The airport security, the tension about getting your luggage and making connecting flights is just too much. So you stop traveling by air. At this point, you still feel okay going to work and doing local errands, but other than that, you start staying home more and more. Then you begin to notice that you're also anxious at work, and then anxious while running errands. You become anxious about being anxious. Eventually this can reach a point where you quit your job and even stop leaving your house altogether. At this point, you have developed a full-blown psychological disorder known as agoraphobia. Avoidance of anxiety has now restricted you to such an extent that your life has become radically circumscribed.

Do you think such a strategy is effective? Even apart from how it warps someone's life, do you think the person with agoraphobia experiences less anxiety by trying to avoid having it? In fact, that's not the case: people with this disorder are *more* frightened than they were before they started avoiding things, not less. The rest of us experience some anxiety when we travel or go to work. But then, we don't *expect* to have no anxiety at all. We *accept* a certain level of anxiety as being okay. By accepting the anxiety, our lives stay open.

When you try to avoid thoughts and feelings, you're back with the flying pigs. The only thing to do about flying pigs is let it be okay to think about them. Once you decide it's okay, you end up not thinking about them very much at all, because you no longer define thinking about them as a problem.

Secret Bargains

There's an important point here: you must really be *willing* to have these uncomfortable thoughts and feelings. If you try to fool yourself into thinking it's okay to be aware of them, but are really just pretending so you can avoid them, you're making a secret bargain; you're still just trying to avoid and suppress.

My clients betray this hidden agenda frequently. They return after a week of practicing being mindful of what they are experiencing, only to tell me it "didn't work." When I ask how they know this, the secret bargain becomes apparent. "Working" means not having the unpleasant thoughts and feelings, which means they're still trying to finesse the situation using avoidance and suppression.

Many of us wonder from time to time if we remembered to close the garage door or left the coffeepot on when we left the house. But if we try to *avoid* thinking such thoughts, we create an inner battle. We could even develop obsessive-compulsive disorder, which is exactly characterized by the struggle against such unwanted thoughts.

People with a history of depression might try to avoid having depressed thoughts. Every time a sad thought or feeling arises, they worry. They fear the depression is coming back. That's such an awful experience that they would do almost anything to avoid having it return. So they try not to acknowledge sad thoughts. But the more they try not to have them, the more they return.

Their very efforts to avoid depression actually increase it. It's only when you're willing to experience things just as they are that the level of unpleasant thoughts and feelings finds a natural balance in the ecology of the psyche. Gradually, you can learn to detect the tension and struggle in you that indicate you've made a secret bargain to avoid having certain feelings, and you learn instead to open to them.

Dealing with inner states is much like dealing with a young child who demands your attention by coming to you, tugging at your sleeve, and saying, "Come look what I can do! Look! Look!" If we try to put the child off, he only intensifies his efforts to be seen by tugging harder at us, talking louder, or even starting to whine. The more you try to avoid dealing with the child, the more insistent he becomes. Even if you're reading a wonderful book you don't want to put down, until you stop and acknowledge the child by taking a moment or two to see what he wants you to see, you won't have any peace.

Our thoughts and feelings are just like that young child. They want us to see them, to know them, to experience them. When we try to avoid them, the situation only gets worse.

The psyche wants to be open and free-flowing, moving in harmony with the ever-changing, impermanent world of our experience. But we want a world that's reliable and certain. We want to avoid the discomfort of a world that's always changing and therefore always uncertain. When we try to avoid this, when we resist the ever-changing, impermanent nature of experience, we create blockages. And blockages create havoc. What happens when you have a blockage in your blood flow? It can lead to a heart attack or a stroke. Psychological blockages are equally damaging. The principle is this: always be willing to start with the truth of your actual experience.

You are not helpless before your thoughts and feelings. There are ways to work with them. But above all, maintain good psychic circulation. Start with the truth.

Tending Your Garden

Your consciousness is a garden. In the garden are many beautiful plants. There are lovely flowers, beautiful trees, and delicious fruits and vegetables. These beautiful manifestations correspond to the healing energies in your consciousness, energies like kindness, wisdom, happiness, joy, and serenity. But no matter how diligent a gardener you are, from time to time weeds spring up as well. Inevitably, our kindness, wisdom, happiness, and serenity aren't the only things that grow in our gardens. Anger, sadness, irritation, despair, grief, and hopelessness manifest as well.

As every gardener knows, the surface of your garden isn't the whole story. Belowground lie all kinds of seeds. Some of them are the seeds of beautiful flowers, lovely plants of all kinds that can surprise and gladden us. But there are also many unpleasant seeds that don't make us so happy.

One spring, I started a new vegetable garden by preparing the ground with a rototiller to loosen the compacted soil. By doing this, however, I also churned up all the dormant seeds in the ground. That summer, it seemed all I did was weed the garden so that my lettuce and tomato plants would have a chance.

Some life events are like using a rototiller. Great difficulties in life churn up difficult emotions that we didn't know were there or that we thought we'd already dealt with. Suffering a major loss stirs up all the previous losses you've experienced. You might get discouraged if you thought all that old pain was gone forever. But wise gardeners are prepared: they know there are many kinds of seeds lying dormant in the garden, awaiting the chance to manifest.

Fortunately, difficult events can also bring up some wonderful surprises. We might also discover some courage, fortitude, patience, or kindness we hadn't imagined we had. But whether or not such qualities bloom in us, many difficult thoughts, feelings, and memories will all but certainly come up as we endure a major loss, setback, illness, or other devastating event.

The most important practice is to be a good gardener, to take good care of your consciousness so that wonderful plants have a chance to manifest and stay around as long as possible, and so that the less wonderful plants won't be around as much. You can tend your garden in such a way that the beautiful, wise, and true elements within you manifest, and so that the less beautiful elements in you become less prevalent.

The most important thing you can do to take care of your garden of consciousness is to make sure your garden has plenty of sunshine and water.

The Sunlight of Awareness

After the long night, a flower may be completely closed when the morning sun rises. But gradually, as sunlight continues to penetrate the flower, the flower can't resist. It has to open up, revealing its full beauty and radiance.

The kind of sunlight our consciousness requires to bloom is called mindfulness. When our mindfulness shines on the beautiful flowers of kindness, wisdom, peace, and happiness, those things open up, manifest, and shine forth. It's like the lyrics of the children's song that says, "If you're happy and you know it, clap your hands." If you are happy and know you're happy, if you are happy and mindful of your happiness, you have even greater happiness. When we shine the light of mindfulness on the lovely plants in our gardens, they thrive. They reveal themselves and flourish, staying around much longer than they otherwise would.

Mindfulness has another important quality. Every time we shine the sunlight of our awareness on our difficult emotions, they lose strength. The more we allow ourselves to hold our sadness, our worry, and our anger in mindfulness, the more workable these elements become. And they will also manifest less often, less powerfully, and for a shorter duration.

Water the Flowers, Not the Weeds

If you're out watering your flower garden by hand, you naturally concentrate the flow of water to benefit your beautiful flowers. If there's an area of weeds, you don't waste water there. As best you can, you avoid watering the weeds.

It's the same with your consciousness. You can learn to selectively water the positive seeds and flowers in you by attending to them. There are enough weeds. You don't have to encourage them.

To encourage beneficial mental states, seek experiences that stimulate them and avoid unnecessary experiences that encourage harmful ones. When you encounter something positive and healing, pause with it, lighting the lamp of your mindfulness to savor and appreciate it. If you notice the wonderful smell of the rain, for example, instead of just moving quickly past the experience without deeply appreciating it, you can prolong your contact with this wonderful sensation. Pause for a moment and really let yourself experience the smell of the rain. If you are struck by the blueness of the sky, linger for a moment and breathe mindfully, taking in the wonderful blue color. Don't rush past these marvelous experiences, treating them as if they are unimportant. To treat them as unimportant is ultimately to treat yourself as unimportant. This is your life: enjoy it!

Sometimes, we unwittingly encourage the weeds within us. We voluntarily expose ourselves to toxic and destructive things. When we're sad, we tend to feed the sadness by playing sad music, drinking too much, and rehearsing our sad thoughts internally and to anyone who can bear listening to us.

Protect yourself from experiences that harm your consciousness. Some movies, television shows, books, magazines, and even conversations can encourage the negative seeds within you. It's important to notice how things actually affect you and not let them colonize your consciousness, even if they're popular or critics say they're artistic. If you see this clearly, you won't want to continue exposing yourself to this kind of experience. There are many lovely things in the world. Why focus so much on the potentially destructive ones?

Raise Mindfulness

For teaching purposes, we can distinguish between two ways of being mindful that bring healing to our pain: mere recognition and deep embracing.

Mere Recognition

When we experience the energy of painful emotions, we need to raise another kind of energy within us to take care of these feelings. This second kind of energy is the energy of mindfulness. We practice *mere recognition*, just noticing what's there. Invoke a feeling of interest and friendly curiosity about what you're feeling: "What is this? What am I experiencing in my body, in my mind?" Notice the kind of thinking that's coming up. Notice the emotions that are present. Notice the sensations in your body associated with these thoughts and feelings. Breathe. Practice just being willing to be with them. Let your awareness reflect exactly what's there, like a still, clear mountain lake. Since you know that these are thoughts and feelings, and that, like everything else, they will come up for a while, stay for a while, and then disappear, you don't have to fear them, even if they're unpleasant. You can breathe in and out with these thoughts and feelings and be present to them, using phrases like these:

- Breathing in and out, I know there's a sad feeling here.

- Breathing in and out, I know there's a feeling of anger.

- Breathing in and out, I know a thought is arising that the situation is hopeless.

- Breathing in and out, I know there's a tightness in my stomach.

It's important to notice how these observations are worded. You don't practice mere recognition by telling yourself, "I'm angry!" or "I'm sad!" or "It's hopeless!" When you say, "I'm angry," you identify with the feeling. You are fused with it, embedded in it, as though all there is to you is anger. You and anger are the same thing. But when you tell yourself, "There's anger here," you open up a zone of freedom. You create some space between yourself and the emotion. You can see that the anger is present as a kind of energy in your body and mind, but you have the chance to remember that you are not only anger. You know the anger is neither permanent nor personal. You know that you are more than your anger, even if anger is dominating your experience at the moment.

In the same way, say to yourself, "I am having a thought that this is terrible," not just, "This is terrible!" When you tell yourself, "This is terrible!" it seems like ultimate truth. You don't question it. But when you mindfully notice what's happening, when you tell yourself, "I am having the thought that this is terrible," you know that this is just a thought. It could be true, untrue, or somewhere in between. But you don't just have to accept it blindly.

Zen teacher Ezra Bayda (2008) suggests that when such a thought arises, we note it by telling ourselves that we're having a *believed* thought that this is unbearable. That wonderful little word "believed" works in a very interesting way. Noting the fact that you believe the thought introduces through the back door the possibility that you might choose *not* to believe it. This is much more skillful than trying to argue with yourself about it and, once again, taking the risk of turning yourself into a battlefield. Then you're fighting between the parts of you that believe something and those that don't, and peace won't issue from struggle. Instead,

Bayda teaches, just add in the word "believed." Let it do the work by itself, without struggling.

Deep Embracing

The first strategy, then, is the practice of just noticing, or mere recognition. You just note what's there without fighting against it. If you are anxious and note that you are anxious, then mindfulness is already present to some degree. As your mindfulness becomes more solid and stable, however, you learn to raise within you a quality of mindfulness that contains a strong element of clarity, serenity, and acceptance. You raise clarity and calm to *embrace* your area of suffering. At first your mindfulness may be easily overwhelmed. But as your practice deepens, mindfulness grows stronger, becoming capable of embracing ever more difficult emotions with serenity. From time to time, you have the realization that something that once overwhelmed your capacity to be present no longer does so. This gives you the encouragement to continue practicing.

To learn to do this, breathe in and out. Touch the aspect of yourself that's calm, serene, and wise. If this is difficult at first, begin by contemplating something that evokes those feelings, like a beautiful lake or mountain. Then you can let go of that image while maintaining the serenity it evokes. And with that energy, you then hold what's going on in a loving and kind embrace. You hold your pain like a mother very tenderly holding her crying baby. She doesn't hold the baby with a repressive energy. She doesn't tell her baby, "Shut up! I can't stand it! Grow up! Act your age!" Nor does she ignore her baby and its pain. Instead, she evokes her own calmness, clarity, and mindfulness to hold the baby patiently, let it cry, and look into the nature of her baby's distress. Sometimes you might even consciously invoke this image of the tender mother to help you embrace your pain in this way and allow a healing attitude to emerge.

To evoke serenity and acceptance, you can also use imagery from your religious heritage. Buddhists have often used images of the Buddha this way. Looking at a calm, beautiful Buddha figure can serve this purpose very effectively. Or you can do the "Touching the Buddha Within" practice from chapter 3.

I once advised a Catholic client that she might do this with an image of Mother Mary. I suggested she contemplate an image of her that expresses calmness and love, and imagine Mary holding her and calming her distress. This worked quite well for her. You can use an image of the bodhisattva Kwan Yin, who embodies compassion, or an image of Christ, a saint, or whatever personifies calmness, kindness, and wisdom. Let this image bring forth the seeds of these qualities in your consciousness. Let it hold your pain.

The serenity of these images reminds us that this process isn't about raising calmness to have it fight against our painful feelings. There's no battle. There's no repression. There's only calm, patient, kind awareness holding our distress. You don't force it, just as when you cut your finger you don't force the cells to repair the damage. You only take care of the wound by cleaning it and protecting it. You don't bring the healing. You just create the causes and conditions for healing to happen by itself.

It's instructive to use this practice to help with minor emotional disturbances at first. When you do this, you gain a lot of confidence. You gain faith in the practice and a firsthand knowledge of its effectiveness. Larger emotional disturbances may be more difficult, but the same principles apply. They just require more patience and persistence, in the form of your gently and repeatedly returning to take care of your pain. If you have gained strength from working with smaller difficulties, you will have the necessary insight. But if you haven't tried this with less intense emotions, you might not remember to use this practice when more intense ones arise.

As your mindfulness grows stronger, you experience greater resilience in the face of life's obstacles, both the daily difficulties and the major changes. You recognize that things that used to bother you a great deal don't disturb you as much or as long. However, please don't imagine that you have failed if a strong emotion overwhelms you for a while, even in some cases for days, weeks, or longer. If the pain is too strong and too persistent, a therapist can help you hold it in a healing therapeutic environment. This, too, is no failure. Advanced mindfulness practitioners can be overwhelmed sometimes, even if it happens less frequently. Ultimately, the only failure is not practicing. Waste no time by adding self-recriminations to such difficult experiences, but instead, as soon as you can, raise the serene, kind, accepting energy of mindfulness.

Administer the Antidote

The clarity and calmness of mindfulness provide a general strategy for healing painful emotional states. Mindfulness calms our agitated emotions. By holding them in its embrace, we gradually find our way through all difficulties. But there are also more specific strategies we can use from Buddhist teachings. In addition to using mindfulness as a general remedy, we can use a more specific approach. We can administer the antidote.

For example, if you experience a feeling of hatred or anger, the antidotes are love and compassion. To do this practice, strongly remind yourself that the person you're angry at is, like you, only trying to be happy and avoid suffering. That person's actions are an attempt to do just that, even if his notion of what will accomplish this is very distorted. There must be some energy behind this insight, but if you see this clearly enough, your anger will diminish.

"If we could read the secret history of our enemies, we should see sorrow and suffering enough to disarm all hostility," wrote

Longfellow (2000, 797). Being alive involves many wonderful experiences that are always available to us. But this doesn't mean there aren't also many difficulties. A good use of these difficulties is to let them teach us compassion. We *know* what it's like to suffer. We *know* what it's like to be less than our best, to end up saying and doing unwise or even destructive things. If we know this about ourselves with sufficient clarity, we can use this knowledge to maintain compassion toward others. It only requires some training.

We can use the teaching of impermanence to defuse our anger. When you are angry at someone, envision that person as she will be a long time into the future, when both of you are already long dead. Realizing that, like you, the other person will then just be bones or dust helps you see the situation through the lens of eternity. If you can see this clearly enough, deeply enough, your anger will vanish.

If a feeling of sadness arises, we can cultivate the antidote by reminding ourselves of what's good in our lives. Touch what's good in your present situation. Touch these things deeply and with concentration. Once again, this isn't a matter of creating a fight within yourself. Nor is it a matter of self-recrimination of this sort: "I have no right to feel sad, because I have all these good things in my life, and others haven't even had these." It's simply a matter of noting the sadness, holding it in mindfulness, and simultaneously raising a different kind of energy. We can raise the energy of happiness or gratitude alongside the sadness and pain, letting the happy feeling naturally take care of the unhappy feeling.

When our sadness is intense, it sometimes contains an element of alienation, of separation, a sense of being all alone and lost in our sorrow. We feel as though no one has ever suffered what we are suffering, endured what we are enduring. That feeling is a delusion, but sometimes a very strong one. When that's the case, think of all the people in the world who are suffering from the same kind of difficulty you are experiencing, and send light and kindness to them all. A woman who has miscarried can radiate kindness to all the women who have been through that experience. Someone who is getting divorced can radiate kindness to the many people who have endured such sorrows. Even if sadness has come up for no apparent reason, we can radiate kindness toward all the people who have experienced sadness arising for no reason. This way, we immediately feel a little better. Even if the sadness is still present, it's already a little different. For now it's a sadness that *connects* us to other people, instead of one that cuts us off from them.

So what kind of energy would you raise if you felt envious? Say your friend has a better car or house. Or you are a manager and learn that a colleague is being honored or has won a large grant. Maybe you're a writer who finds out your friend's book has become a best seller. Since you are a human being, you may well have feelings like "Why isn't it me? Why am I not the one who is experiencing such things?"

Mindfulness is always about acknowledging the truth: "I know what this is. This is envy." "A feeling of envy is here." Once you know this, you recognize that this is a painful state to be in, not one you want to foster. Certainly you know it's natural and you don't need to punish yourself, especially since, as I've mentioned, thoughts like these arise of their own accord. But we can deeply consider how fortunate this person is, how much we would enjoy having what she has, and how good this must feel for her. Also, if we know something about the other person's life difficulties, we can be particularly glad that something good has come her way. In other words, this is a kind of no-self practice, wherein we learn to see the good that befalls others as essentially no different from the good that befalls us, knowing that their happiness and ours are interconnected. After all, if good can happen to someone else, it can happen to us as well.

Similarly, if you feel shame or embarrassment, remember the best of who you are, your good qualities and accomplishments. Remember your Buddha nature. If you feel disappointment, raise a feeling of gratitude by recalling good things in your life. We can take care of every painful emotional state by finding an antidote, using our wisdom and clarity to invoke it and let it do the work of healing without our having to struggle.

The Two Steps of Emotional Care

In essence, there are two steps to caring for our emotions: mindfully acknowledge what you're feeling and experiencing, and then take care of these emotions. A lot of unnecessary pain results from incorrectly practicing one or the other of these two steps, or from neglecting one of them altogether.

Steve and Karin

Steve runs his own sporting goods store, and many people consider him resilient and successful. When difficulties come up in his business, he stays squarely in problem-solving mode, never letting himself get stuck in his emotions. Steve comes into therapy, however, because while this way of being in the world works for him in some ways, he notices it doesn't work in others. What works in his business life doesn't work so well in his relationships. For this reason, he lacks close friends and a life partner, both of which are very important to him.

Karin has the opposite difficulty. A successful attorney in a prominent law firm, she has to deal with lots of people in a large organization. The organization does not consistently support Karin. Every time she receives a comment that's anything less than glowing praise for her work, she becomes thoroughly dispirited. This stresses not only her work life but also her personal life, because friends and partners have quickly burned out on her emotional ups and downs.

It might seem obvious that Steve's problem lies with the first step, mindfully acknowledging his feelings, while he has no problem with the second one, taking care of the emotions. He's very busy fixing, taking care of difficult situations. But he runs so quickly past the emotional aspects of problems that he hardly lets himself be aware of what's going on with him. He appears to cope well, and that looks like strength on the surface. But he avoids what he's actually feeling. Because he's not fully in touch, his coping will ultimately be off base as well. His inability to acknowledge vulnerable feelings reduces his capacity for intimacy, since the ability to reveal vulnerability is a crucial ingredient in being close.

While Karin's coping style is quite different from Steve's, she also has a problem with the first step. She knows strong emotions are present but gets completely engulfed in them anyway. She's aware, in a way, but not *mindful*. She isn't holding her emotions in her awareness, but is being swept away by them. Because she gets so violently tossed by her emotional storms, she never gets to the second step, taking care of her emotions. She never even begins to ask herself, "What can I do to help myself? How can I take care of these feelings?"

While Steve and Karin appear to be very different, in actuality both are deficient in taking the first step, mindfully acknowledging what they're feeling. Steve barely lets himself know he's feeling anything, while Karin gets lost in the feelings. Neither of these is what's meant by mindfulness of emotion. If a therapist told Karin she needed to be mindful of her feelings, she'd laugh. All she does is experience her feelings, she might say. But indeed, she isn't really *mindful* of them—she's *lost* in them. Mindfulness is learning to be in the middle path between denial, on the one hand, and hysteria or fusion on the other. Mindfulness means to know the truth without getting lost in it, remembering that thoughts and feelings are impermanent and selfless: they don't last, and they're not you.

Steve and Karin react as they do, in part, because of the stories they hold about themselves. Steve sees himself as a tough, no-nonsense businessman. He has no time for useless emotions. What do they accomplish anyway? To him, to feel emotion means weakness. Karin, on the other hand, sees herself as weak. Because she sees herself this way, every time a strong emotion arises, she interprets it as more evidence of her weakness. She gets stuck and becomes the victim of her feelings.

When we see this with the eyes of impermanence and no self, we realize that the ideas Karin and Steve have of themselves are fables. If Steve pays closer attention, he will see that he feels vulnerable at times, as all of us do. Such feelings come and go, as do his feelings of strength and competence. That doesn't make him weak or strong, just human.

Karin also experiences feelings of strength as well as vulnerable feelings. But because her self-story is that she's weak, her experience of strength and competence scarcely registers. Whenever she notices a vulnerable feeling, her fear and avoidance make it stronger. And the small wave of feeling quickly turns into a tsunami, wiping out all her positive sense of self.

When we are mindful, we stay in the middle: We see that thoughts come and go, and know that none of them are, in the deepest and fullest sense, reality. All are one-sided and partial. There's no such thing as a person who never feels vulnerable, afraid, lonely, or sad. But if we know that such feelings are the result of natural processes and that they're not the ultimate truth of who we are and how the world is, we can survive. We don't need to let them wash away all feelings of happiness and well-being.

Follow the Steps

The first step, then, is to let yourself know what you're actually experiencing. Raise mindfulness through mere recognition and clear, serene awareness to see just exactly what's happening. Let mindfulness hold and embrace the feelings you're having. Only after you have let yourself clearly experience what's going on should you move on to the second step. Take your time with this. Being aware helps you know when the emotions are too strong for you to safely act. Wait until you have some calm, some clarity, before speaking or acting. Hasty and impulsive words and actions seldom help.

Sometimes people get the idea that mindfulness is a passive practice. But this is far from the truth. It's just that, when we live mindfully, we act from clarity and depth. Otherwise, when our emotions get hooked, we think of many things to say and do that would only make the situation worse. Often our first impulse is a destructive one. But when we are deeply and clearly in touch with what's happening, our action grows naturally out of that awareness. When we act from this base, from a base of clarity and calm, our actions are more on target. Less of what we do and say will cause ourselves and others to suffer. Actions based on mindfulness have a sense of rightness about them.

In baseball, they say the most important pitch is strike one, meaning that it helps if the first pitch is a strike. In the same way, the first step is the key. If we get it right, if our contact with what's happening is deep enough, neither repressed nor embedded, the second step will grow naturally out of the first. We'll know what to do and what to avoid doing. Once we have established calmness and clarity, we see what we can do to improve the situation and feel better. When we can be in touch and aware, and act effectively out of that awareness, we become empowered and experience relief and healing.

Interrupt Repetitive Thinking

Part of the second step, taking care of our emotions, is to interrupt our tendency to ruminate on our difficulties and get lost in them. To interrupt rumination, we engage in some activity. Such activities are of two kinds: either things that give us a sense of *mastery*, a sense of accomplishment; or pleasurable things that create a lot of involvement, a sense of *flow*.

Mastery is about getting things done. If your bills have gone unpaid for a while or your house needs to be cleaned, your garden tended, a phone call made, you will feel better after accomplishing one of these tasks and crossing it off your to-do list. The feeling of accomplishment, of getting unstuck concerning tasks you have put off, can give you a direct lift. Not only do you feel the relief of getting it done, but also, while you're doing the task, you're not rehearsing your worries. You prevent your emotions from growing stronger and cycling into ever more painful states.

Flow experiences are activities that involve you completely and match your skill level. It doesn't have to be any particular activity. For example, you might experience flow while playing Ping-Pong or tennis. When well matched with an opponent, you can get completely engrossed in the game. There's no time for thoughts and worries to surface. You have to concentrate and respond very quickly, so you are alive in the present moment.

Sometimes such activities are called distractions, meaning they distract you from your painful emotional states. But during the activities themselves, if they are to be maximally effective, you should be anything but distracted. The more involving they are, the better. So concentrate. See about giving the task at hand your full attention.

If you are prone toward depressive or other kinds of painful emotional states, it helps to prepare a list of mastery and flow activities ahead of time. When you are already sad or worried, it can be more difficult to think of what to do. Having a list already prepared can make the difference between your being able to act, on the one hand, and getting stuck in a mood state, on the other.

Once you have completed your activity, check in with your emotions. Often, they will be less overwhelming. At the very least, you can observe that they have a different quality. In this way, you confirm the impermanent nature of thoughts and feelings.

Psychologists like to rate things, and this can be a mindfulness practice in itself. If you enjoy thinking like a scientist, rate your level of distress from 0 to 10 before and after your activity. This can help you be mindful of subtle changes. If your sadness decreases from 6 to 5, the numerical rating can help you detect this small change more easily than if you only notice you are somewhat sad before the activity and still somewhat sad afterward.

By paying attention to the effects of your activity, you also learn which activities help the most. Then you can choose the most powerful ones when you need them, and avoid those that aren't as useful. This is an important part of caring for the garden of your consciousness.

Taking Care of Your Consciousness: A Summary

Since caring for your consciousness is so important, I have summarized the strategies in this chapter so you can refer to them more easily. Consult this summary whenever you are in distress, and put one or more elements into practice.

- *Remember* that your mental contents are shaping your perceptions more than you imagine. If you're in distress, the situation is probably less bleak than it seems.

- Practice *mere recognition*. Don't suppress. Don't avoid. Acknowledge what you're experiencing, noting your thoughts, emotions, and bodily sensations: "There's a feeling of _____ here." "I'm having a believed thought that _____." "I'm aware of feeling _____ in my body." Breathe mindfully during these experiences.

- *Practice deep embracing.* Use images that evoke seren- ity (a beautiful lake or mountain, a tree or flower, an image of the Buddha or Christ, and so on) to evoke calm, accepting wisdom in your awareness. Let this aspect hold your area of pain like a tender, loving mother holding her infant.

- Practice *awareness of positive elements* in your life before difficulties arise so you can be more resilient when they do.

- Practice *psychological defense.* Protect yourself, when possible, from excessive exposure to psychological toxins in your environment.

- *Raise the antidote.* For anger, evoke love and compas- sion; for sadness, happiness; for agitation and worry, serenity; for envy, sympathetic joy, letting yourself feel the other person's happiness as if it were your own.

- *Follow the two steps* in sequence of mindfully recogniz- ing what you feel and taking care of your emotions. Make sure you acknowledge your actual feeling before you try to cope by getting perspective on the situation or taking action.

- *Radiate kindness* to all who suffer from a situation similar to the one that's making you suffer so you can end isolation or alienation.

- *Interrupt repetitive thinking* by engaging in activities that are intrinsically rewarding or that give you a sense of accomplishment.

- *Confirm impermanence.* Note how the feeling changes over time. For example, rate the strength of your painful feeling on a scale of 0 to 10 before and after an activity.

chapter 5

Self, No Self, and Other

The moment you see how important it is to love yourself, you will stop making others suffer.

—Buddha

On the surface, our culture appears very self-centered. We seem devoted to our own satisfaction. We are encouraged everywhere to love ourselves and be assertive about stating our needs. We want only the most fulfilling relationships and careers. We want nice clothes, beautifully decorated homes, the best coffee beans, luxury cars, fabulous vacations, and the best equipment—even for activities we seldom engage in. Ours is clearly a culture in the *kamadhatu*, the realm of desire.

Yet ironically, when we look just past the surface, it's easy to see that we aren't actually very good at loving ourselves, being kind to ourselves, and holding ourselves in genuine esteem. Our excessive display of self-centeredness barely conceals an underlying self-hatred.

Every psychotherapist has had the experience of working with people whose difficulties center largely on a deficit of self-love. Marcy is a good example.

Refusing the Gift: Marcy's Story

Marcy's a natural caregiver. She's a devoted nurse and a dedicated wife, daughter, and mother. Her husband's an attorney, with a larger than life personality. Everything in the household centers on his needs. Between her work, her children, and her demanding husband, Marcy feels continually drained and distressed. She's forever trying to take care of everyone around her. With little capacity to take care of herself, Marcy never asks for help or consideration. She's afraid to ask for what she wants.

A poignant childhood memory reveals the deep roots of her lack of self-love. When she was five years old, her father uncharacteristically took her shopping and offered to buy her whatever toy she wanted. Little Marcy could only shake her head mutely. She couldn't accept the gift. Somehow the very thought of it terrified her. In accord with their fundamentalist religion, her parents had continually taught her to put others first. It felt dangerous to accept her father's offer.

When her aging mother is diagnosed with lung cancer, Marcy scarcely hesitates; she takes her mother into her home immediately. She even quits her job to dedicate herself to her mother's care. Though outwardly she continues doing everything for her mother and her family, inwardly she seethes with resentment and anger. Yet at the same time, it's difficult for her to imagine doing things any other way. It's so deeply ingrained in her to think of others that she can scarcely imagine thinking of herself or even considering alternative ways of getting her mother the care she needs.

If Marcy were happy in her caregiver role, you could argue that there's no problem with it. If that's how someone wants to spend her life, if she finds meaning in living this way and feels happy doing it, who could say she shouldn't? It might not be the way others would choose to live, but if it works for her, it's fine.

The problem is, it doesn't work for her. She finds herself perpetually miserable and angry. She is making a choice, but would never think of it as such, for there's no experience of freedom in her decision—only compulsive duty. Marcy needs to learn to either get more comfortable advocating for herself, nourishing herself, and taking care of her well-being, or release her anger and resentment and accept the situation with an open heart. The worst possible outcome would be for her to continue putting others ahead of herself while resenting it deeply.

Self and Other

You may recall from chapter 2 that the Buddha offered us a radically different way of seeing who we are: the way of no self. He taught that rather than existing as separate, unchanging entities, we are constantly changing streams of energy. We are profoundly interconnected with everything in the cosmos.

The Buddha offered the insight of no self to free us, to help us realize the truth of deep connectedness and find a truer vision of the way things really are. Love is the natural and inevitable consequence of this insight. If you are interconnected to everything and everyone, what sense would it make to be anything other than kind? To hurt another is to hurt yourself.

But there's a tendency in religious and spiritual teaching to misuse such insights. Though in the realm of ultimate truth there's no separate self, there *is* a certain relative truth to being a self, a unique individual, separate from others, with your own needs, desires, abilities, and inclinations. If we try to bypass this level, we can end up as miserable as Marcy.

My mother recounted that as a child, she sometimes labored diligently over her homework, only to have her envious older sister destroy it. Whenever she complained to her mother, a religious woman with fundamentalist leanings, her mother responded, "The good one doesn't complain." This is a poisonous use of the teachings on love. How devastating to a child to realize that her own mother wouldn't help her in this unjust situation! This is an example of getting bit by the snake of religion. It's an abdication of parental responsibility, an attempt to bypass the psychological level in the name of religion.

Buddhist teacher Achaan Chah once found that one of his students hadn't repaired the roof of his hut when the wind had blown it off. It was the rainy season, and the rain came streaming in on him in torrents. After several days of this, he asked the student why he didn't repair his hut. The student said he was practicing not clinging. "This is not clinging without wisdom," commented Achaan Chah. "It is about the same as the equanimity of a water buffalo" (Kornfield 1996, 41).

To be a spiritual person, we must not become something less than human. We must retain and care for our humanness. We must not sacrifice common sense. To do this, we needn't be afraid to use the language of self, even though we know it isn't the ultimate truth of our situation. Marcy clearly needs help with learning to be kinder to herself, so she can stop always putting herself last. My grandmother needed to stand up for her daughter in the face of unjust treatment. The student needed to repair his hut. If we are to be loving and kind, we must include ourselves in the arc of that love and kindness. If we are to learn to love our neighbors as ourselves, then love of neighbor must be built on the solid foundation of love of self. We can't pretend otherwise. Only, it must be true self-love, not the superficial and exaggerated selfishness that reveals its lack.

In Marcy's case, we can readily see that a love of others that's not founded on a love of self ends up being neither. Trying to love her family without having kindness for herself ends up looking more like hatred than love. In this, as in many other situations, there's a deep law: when we try too hard to be good, we often end up doing harm instead. Marcy's "love" is not really love at all. If she can't love herself, she can't love others either.

At this relative level of analysis, we can consider that a balance needs to be struck between love of others and love of self:

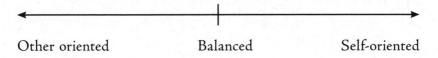

Other oriented   Balanced   Self-oriented

If we are too far to the left, too centered on others, we end up being miserable. And when we are miserable, that in turn affects everyone around us. The people we try to help instead feel our resentment and anger, which plants unwholesome seeds in the garden of their consciousness as well as our own.

People who are other oriented fear that this means they have to move radically to the right. But they don't need to suddenly become selfish. That would conflict too much with their view of themselves, and with their desire to be kind and loving. And in fact, this concern is chimerical, because there's little actual danger that would happen with those who have a strong habit of thinking about others. Their danger isn't in becoming selfish; it's in remaining unkind to themselves and consequently spreading their unhappiness and resentment unintentionally.

Less obviously, at the opposite end of the scale, self-oriented people are also unhappy. Preoccupation with self creates a constant tension to monitor the environment for injustice, for any hint that they might be receiving less than their entire due. And since their idea of fairness is highly skewed toward themselves and their own needs and desires, they often perceive this to be the case. That's why narcissistic individuals have a tendency toward explosive anger and rage. The world always seems unfair to them.

A strong self-orientation also creates very distorted relationships. On the one hand, such individuals often end up being angry at others for being insufficiently cooperative with their self-centered agenda. This often results in relationships coming to an abrupt end. On the other hand, they may attract people who are passive, who have difficulty advocating for themselves. Takers attract givers. But this, too, is far from a happy complementarity. Both become angry. The givers end up feeling resentful, as Marcy did. And ironically, so do the takers. Even though they receive more than is fair, their distorted perception causes them to see the situation as unfair to them, while the givers' anger appears to them as completely unwarranted selfishness.

Finding a balance between self and other isn't just a matter of being exactly in the middle of the spectrum in every moment. It's a balance *across time*. A person with a good self-other balance is flexible. She puts herself first—*at times*. And she puts others first—*at times*. The parent who wakes up in the middle of the night and hears his infant crying knows that this is a time to put the child's needs first, even though he needs his own sleep too. Likewise, a social worker, doctor, or psychotherapist who focuses on others all day needs to find ways to rebalance, to take care of herself at other times, nourishing seeds of happiness and well-being in herself to keep from becoming depleted and angry.

People like Marcy have made an unspoken pact with the world. They behave selflessly, while harboring the secret expectation that, since they are so devoted to others, others will in turn take care of them without their even needing to ask. There are at least two problems with this pact: First of all, the world never agreed to it; the pact exists only for them. And second, in practice such a pact is an expectation that others will read their minds, somehow automatically knowing what they want and need without their having to express it. As infants, before we could talk and express our needs, there was no other choice. But as adults, this is a poor strategy. Others will always be more aware of their own thoughts and feelings than they will be of ours. This is the nature of our biology. So the result is anger, the feeling that the world isn't living up to the bargain it actually never made.

More Blessed to Give?

Many are familiar with Christ's teaching that it's more blessed to give than to receive. This is, first of all, a simple statement of fact. During the holidays, aren't we, in fact, often more excited about the gifts we give others than those we receive? The act of giving makes us happy—blessed, in biblical usage.

At the same time, we can ask, when is a gift a gift? A gift is a gift when it's *received*. Unless someone can also receive, the circle of giving isn't complete. Loving is a matter of countless transactions of giving and receiving, receiving and giving. For this to work, we must be able to receive as well as give; we must be able to accept the gift.

There's a story about someone who is given a tour of hell. He sees people in a wonderful room with a lavish banquet before them. It would seem like heaven rather than hell, except for one catch: the people in the room have incredibly long arms with forks on the end of them instead of hands. But since their arms are so long, it's impossible for them to feed themselves. So they sit at the marvelous banquet, hungry and miserable. Asking to see heaven, the visitor is brought to a nearby room. Surprisingly, the situation is the same. It's the same lovely room, the same lavish banquet, and the people have the same long arms. But in this room, there's one crucial difference: the people are feeding each other. Heaven, in other words, is the place where there is love and kindness. But for love and kindness to work, there must be receiving as well as giving.

As a child, Marcy had so internalized the message of being for others that she couldn't receive the gift. This ensures that she inhabits a hell realm in her daily life, even though heaven is available to her and isn't all that far away.

Finding Balance

Finding balance means to find both an outer balance between love of self and love of other, and an inner emotional balance that makes our love true love, regardless of whether it's for self or other.

Hillel's Questions

Rabbi Hillel, the first century BCE teacher who is considered the founder of the rabbinic movement in Judaism, expressed the balance between self and others in his famous three questions:

> *If I am not for myself, who will be for me?*
> *And if I am not for others, what am I?*
> *And if not now, when?*
>   (Quoted in Buxbaum 2004, 268–70)

The order of the questions isn't arbitrary. The first question comes first and *must* come first. It indicates that if we aren't for ourselves, we can't expect anyone else to be either. Being for ourselves, loving and nurturing ourselves, isn't optional. It's a sacred duty. Loving ourselves is the foundation. Since you are a child of the most high, to treat yourself unkindly is a violation.

But Hillel doesn't stop there. He refuses to choose between love of self and love of others. Both count. Both are essential. To be only for yourself is not enough. We also have a responsibility to take care of others. For they, too, are children of the most high, no less than ourselves.

Finally, the third question teaches that our sacred duty to self and others can't be put off. If we are other centered, we must not delay in learning to nurture ourselves. And if we are self-centered, we can't procrastinate. We need to start acting in the interest of others as well, and shouldn't imagine we can wait until tomorrow. Who knows what tomorrow will bring?

The Brahmavihāras

The Buddhist teaching of the Brahmavihāras is another way to think about balance—in this case, the emotional balance inherent in true love. The term *Brahmavihāra* comes from two Sanskrit words, *Brahma*, meaning "God" or "the ultimate," and *vihāra*, meaning "a dwelling place." One who practices this teaching is seen as dwelling with God, living in the ultimate dimension, the kingdom of heaven, the pure land of the Buddha.

What could produce such a wonderful result? There are four elements: love (*maitri*), compassion (*karuna*), joy (*mudita*), and equanimity (*upeksha*). Love is our intention that others have happiness and the causes of happiness. Rather than just an empty wish, this also includes our having the skill necessary to help others be happy. The Sanskrit term *maitri* is related to "friend." So this is the kind of love you have for friends, wishing them happiness in the same way you wish it for yourself. According to the second-century Buddhist sage Nāgārjuna, the practice of love extinguishes anger. Compassion here means our intention that others be free from suffering and the causes of suffering, as well as the requisite skill for making this happen. Nāgārjuna says this practice extinguishes all sorrows and anxieties. Joy involves having the capacity to take pleasure in the good things that happen to yourself and others, without discriminating between the two. Nāgārjuna promises that this practice ends our sadness. Equanimity means evenness of mind, the capacity to let go. Nāgārjuna says that this practice extinguishes our hatred, aversion, and attachment.

These four elements inter-are, and true love contains all of them. If one element is missing, then that isn't true love in its most complete sense.

It's clear enough that true love contains the wish that others and ourselves be happy and free of suffering. But true love also contains joy. You can see this in Marcy's case. There's no joy in her love and service to others. Her help is joyless, full of anger and misery. So her service isn't true love.

Equanimity involves having the capacity to let others be themselves and make their own choices, even if they are unwise, recognizing that we can't make others' decisions for them or alter the consequences of their decisions. Along with love and compassion, equanimity is like what humanistic psychologist Carl Rogers called *nonpossessive warmth* (Rogers 1957). If our warmth is possessive, it isn't love.

Suppose someone gives money to a friend in need—seemingly an act of true love. We can see the element of compassion in not letting someone suffer from want. But what if, later, the giver sees his friend dining in a café he thinks is a little expensive? At this point, the supposed kindness turns to anger. The lack of equanimity, of letting go, reveals that true love wasn't present in the gift.

The Buddha taught that the practice of true love brings many benefits, including sleeping well, feeling light at heart on awakening, avoiding unpleasant dreams, being well liked, being dear to animals, being protected by gods and goddesses, being protected from dangers, easily achieving meditative concentration, having a bright and clear countenance, having a clear mind at the time of death, and being reborn in the Brahma heaven. Clearly the Buddha regarded this practice highly.

Practicing the Brahmavihāras can be very simple. One way is to just bring up the feeling of love and envision yourself radiating it out in all directions to all beings, including yourself. Then in turn, do the same with compassion, joy, and equanimity. At the end of this chapter, you'll find a more detailed way to practice love meditation.

Loving Self and Others Is Not Abstract

Loving ourselves in daily life might seem abstract. When we are told to love ourselves, we often forget that doing so is actually composed of simple, concrete actions. First of all, to love yourself means to pay attention to yourself, to be mindful, and to know what you are feeling and experiencing, without confusing it with what you want to feel or think you should feel. It means experiencing what's actually there. It means taking care of your thoughts, feelings, and bodily sensations by embracing them with mindfulness, as described in chapter 4. It means seeing to it that you stay warm enough in winter and cool enough in summer. It means not letting yourself work to the point of exhaustion, but respecting the limits of your body and mind. To love yourself is to balance stressful experiences and activities with rest and relaxation. Further, it means learning to do all your activities in a stress-free, restful manner. It means doing your best to eat right, take your vitamins, and get enough exercise and rest. Loving yourself means to encourage yourself as a parent would a child. When you do something well, you acknowledge it, giving yourself a mental pat on the back. You tell yourself, "Good job!" and smile to yourself. Loving yourself means that when you do something less than well, when you make a mistake, you treat yourself with kindness and understanding. You look compassionately into any seeds planted in your consciousness to discern the source of any negative impulses so you can do a little better next time. Loving yourself means to notice when your Buddha nature manifests, recognizing that you have grown and changed.

Loving others in daily life is similarly concrete and simple. Loving others means, first of all, to attend to them, to see them, to contemplate the seeds in their gardens with understanding and kindness. When you do this, you will be able to see how you can contribute to other people's happiness, freedom from suffering, and joy. Loving others means cultivating equanimity where they hold different opinions. It means, even with people you have known for many years, not imagining you already understand them fully, but continuing to look deeply into their nature, remembering that other beings are flowing streams, not static, unchanging selves. In this way, you support positive change and growth by allowing yourself to see it and recognize it, rather than assume that because others were a certain way once, they are still that way now. Loving others means giving them the same support and encouragement for positive actions—as well as the same understanding and kindness for less positive actions—that you aspire to give yourself. Loving others means noticing their Buddha nature when it manifests, and nurturing it through that recognition. I wrote a poem about this:

> *While you slept last night, the earth shook.*
> *The guy next door became a buddha.*
> *Today, you see only someone holding a hose,*
> *Cleaning his pickup with sudsy water.*

Always remember that Buddha nature is in you and in everyone around you. Never underestimate yourself or anyone else. Don't define anyone by how they were yesterday, including yourself.

To Love Means to Understand

We use the word "love" in many different ways. We sometimes use it trivially, such as when we say we love hamburgers or we love a certain television program. We use it to express sexual desire. We use it for a strong feeling of affection experienced in the moment, for a sense of dependence or attachment, and for the intention of a lifetime commitment. Perhaps it would be better if we had different words for these things. In New Testament Greek, there are separate words for sexual love (*eros*), the love of friendship (*philos*), and selfless, spiritual love (*agape*). And in the older, classical Greek, there were even more words for specific kinds of love.

Whatever words we use, what is the nature of true love? It's the intention to understand others deeply and kindly. Because they feel understood, psychotherapy clients often feel more deeply loved in sessions than elsewhere, and sometimes more loved than ever before. Therapists don't generally think of themselves as offering love. Indeed, many therapists avoid using such a word, since it can be easily confused with one of its other meanings. But therapists always try to understand. They try to understand without any intention to possess or control. They try to understand unconditionally; that is, they don't intend to understand only as long as clients meet certain conditions, make choices they approve of, or act the way they want them to. Instead, therapists aim to understand even when clients make poor choices and act in ways that aren't conducive to their own well-being. In fact, this is what makes the therapeutic relationship therapeutic.

No wonder people feel loved in therapy. And they aren't wrong to think so. For such understanding is the real nature of love. Outside of therapy, the love we encounter is rife with expectations and conditions. Indeed, this is so much the case that, when people say they love us, we can feel a little uncomfortable or even find ourselves tightening up, wondering what they want from us.

Sometimes we think that what distinguishes the quality of our love is the object of our love, that is, the person we love. We love the person because he or she is so special. We even imagine such love to be of a higher nature because of its particularity. But such love is more about an image that we create of the other person than about the other person per se. Such love can turn to hatred overnight and often does, revealing its true nature. Real love is the intention to understand and go on understanding, even when it's difficult.

If you say you love someone but you don't understand that person, this is probably more some form of attachment than love. To understand someone, however, isn't always easy. To understand is an ongoing, deep intention. It means that even when we don't understand, we are willing to stay open, to continue contemplating all the seeds in the garden of the other's consciousness until we do. It means still remaining open even when we think we understand, rather than stopping at our current level of understanding. It means continuing to contemplate the person so we can reach ever deeper levels of understanding.

Often when we consider another person, all we really perceive is our own habit energy sprouting up into our awareness. Because someone acted a certain way once, we perceive the person the same way now. We assimilate everything he says and does into the view of him we developed earlier. We find ourselves liking or disliking someone we just met because, without our conscious awareness, she looks like someone else we once knew. But perceptions rooted in the past distort what's going on now.

It's said that when the pickpocket sees a saint, all he sees are the saint's pockets. We see others through the distorting lens of our desires and fears. Even if we encountered a perfect buddha, we might not recognize her, but see her only in terms of past encounters and our own general expectations of others.

When we love, we know that we are like other people in wanting to be happy and avoid suffering. Like us, their ideas about what will bring this result may be based on misperceptions. But we have the same basic goals, the same basic nature. True love isn't based on pride or ego, not because absence of ego is morally superior but because true love grows out of unity. When we see the no self, nonseparate nature of other beings, we know love is simply the only thing to do, the only thing that makes sense.

Mindfulness Is Kindness

Mindfulness is the heart of kindness. When you practice mindfulness of the body, you are practicing kindness toward the body. When you practice mindfulness of your thoughts and feelings, you are practicing kindness toward your thoughts and feelings. When you are mindful of another person, you are practicing kindness toward that person. To be seen, to be recognized as existing, to be known in depth, to be understood—this is the nature of love and kindness.

To speak mindfully is to speak kindly. This means not creating dissension by saying things that might be untrue or destructive, no matter how juicy they are. Remaining mindful of the habit energy in you that compels you to pass along tantalizing hearsay teaches you to acknowledge that energy, slow down the process, and avoid spreading hurtful tales.

Powerful habit energies condition our speaking and listening. Distressed parents often find themselves reacting quickly, saying and doing the same ineffective things their own parents did. If someone says something that hurts our feelings, an angry rejoinder can pop out of us reflexively, without our conscious participation. Such responses, of course, only make the situation worse.

When we aren't clear about what we really feel, we give mixed messages. Often the second message is conveyed nonverbally. Saying "How interesting!" while checking the time gives a mixed message. If we tell someone we have time to talk, but reply in an impatient tone, we're giving a mixed message. Mindfulness includes being aware of our tone and gestures, knowing that people often respond more to these characteristics than verbal content.

You can learn to listen deeply and mindfully. You can learn to breathe and smile while listening. You can learn to speak from the center of your being, letting others see you and be seen by you. This doesn't mean you have to always talk about deep topics. Even pointing out a beautiful cloud can come from your center, if you are really present and really appreciate that cloud. Kind conversations from the center of our being have great depth and energy, and bring a lot of healing. This is a central practice of happiness.

When Others Hurt Us

When someone says or does something that triggers a feeling of sadness or anger, we want to lash out. We think lashing out will make us feel better. But lashing out brings no lasting satisfaction. It can even make us feel worse, for in lashing out, we know we haven't acted in accord with our highest intentions. Lashing out strengthens the seed of anger in our consciousness. Further, it creates a cycle of escalation and retaliation. We strike, they strike back, and we strike again. Each round makes the situation more dangerous, more harmful, and more destructive. Each round gains energy, making it increasingly difficult to stop the cycle.

When you're full of strong emotion, often the best thing to do is say to the other person, "I'm not at my best right now. Let's talk about this tomorrow, after I have had a chance to return to myself." Psychologists call this a time-out, and it's useful in many contexts. The key is to deliver your request for a time-out in a neutral way, free of anger. Let the other person know when you can resume the discussion so you don't leave the person hanging. And when you take your time-out, don't feed the tendency to think of ways to win the argument or come up with witty retorts. Just hold your pain in mindfulness and look deeply into the situation. As your mind clears and stabilizes, you will begin to see the way forward. You'll know what you need to do and what you need to avoid doing.

The words and actions of other people are all the fruit of causes and conditions planted by earlier events and circumstances. Knowing this to be the case, we see people's destructive actions as being similar to natural disasters, like storms, floods, or earthquakes. They are ultimately the result of similarly impersonal no-self forces. Seeing this is very liberating.

"Why did he say that? Why did she do that?" Ultimately, it's because of the pain and sorrow planted previously in the other person's consciousness. While regrettable, it's not a personal affront. It's a storm, a flood, an earthquake.

Love and No Self

At the relative level then, we use words like "self" and "other" as convenient fictions or expedients. And in fact, we must take care to consider this level in our day-to-day dealings, making sure we aren't trying to bypass our psychological and emotional issues in the name of deeper truth. Even if we find it difficult to advocate for ourselves, if we are plagued with guilt whenever we try to do so, it's still absolutely necessary. But we can't rest easy in just caring for ourselves either, as if others don't matter or are less significant than we are. We need to love ourselves deeply *as well* as others, even if we are afraid that if we start caring for others, we'll end up on the losing end. Shifting the balance in whatever direction we need to, whether more toward self or others, requires courage and patience.

At the level of ultimate truth, there's no separation between self and other. As subject and object are one, as up and down are part of the same dimension, as life and death are part of the same process, so self and other can't be teased apart. For this reason, the proper relationship to ourselves and to others is of the same nature: kindness and compassion.

We witness the unity of self and others breaking through in accounts of spontaneous altruism, when people unhesitatingly act to help others without thought or reflection, even putting their own lives at risk. A police officer grabs someone who's about to leap off a cliff, without considering the danger to himself or the potential consequences for his family. A soldier unhesitatingly rushes among flying bullets to retrieve a fallen comrade, intuitively grasping that this action is simply necessary, simply the only thing there is to do. At the level of self and self-preservation, such actions are inexplicable. They only make sense when we recognize in them the spontaneous perception of the reality of no self, of no separation, breaking through into conscious awareness and action.

Even in small, everyday actions, we help each other without thinking about it, by holding the door open for someone we've never seen and won't see again, by giving directions to a total stranger on the street, by smiling at the bank teller, or by letting another driver in the lane ahead of us. These, too, bear witness, albeit less dramatically, to the underlying interconnectedness of life. The insight of no self is nothing foreign. It's not something we need to push into our consciousness. It's an element that's already there, one that only needs to be noticed and strengthened.

In the light of no self, selfless actions are simply intelligent behavior. They represent enlightened awareness breaking through the delusion of separateness. From this perspective, it misses the point to label actions as brave or heroic and bestow medals and honors. It's more than false modesty when our heroes protest that their actions were nothing special, for in that moment, they just knew it was what needed doing. Likewise, it's off the mark to puff ourselves up at our own goodness or feel superior to those we help when we perform an act of kindness. Using kind deeds and speech to create a sense of superiority is rooted in separation and ego, and, though not wrong in a moralistic sense, is incorrect and off base, rooted in delusion. Kind words and actions accord with reality.

Even in moments when the spontaneous perception of unity fails to break through, it helps to act in accord with kindness and compassion. Sometimes we have to change our behavior before our insight changes. When we begin to act strongly, with kindness and compassion, we are mysteriously aided by unseen hands.

Acting with kindness lines us up with reality. It's actually a little funny that in our culture, we think it's hard-nosed financiers or capitalists who are realistic, when actually, their actions are not based on reality at all, but on perceptions of separateness and permanence, on deluded mind. A buddha is the true realist. Kindness accords with enlightened mind. And every time we act in accord with this factor, we open our awareness to see more veridically, to see no self and inter-being, the nonseparate nature of reality.

Science offers some evidence that love is good for us. One example is a study in which college students viewed a film of Mother Teresa caring for Calcutta's poor. Even though some students found the film depressing and Mother Teresa's rigid religiosity off-putting, they still showed an increase in immune response as measured by s-IgA, an immune-boosting hormone found in saliva (McClelland 1986). In another kind of investigation, when a Tibetan monk did loving-kindness meditation in an fMRI, a machine that shows brain functioning in real time, activation dramatically increased in the left part of his middle frontal gyrus, an area of the brain associated with joy and enthusiasm (Barasch 2005). Practicing love makes us happy.

On the other hand, emotions like anger hurt us. When we're angry, our body releases the stress hormones cortisol, epinephrine, and norepinephrine into our bloodstream. These hormones are implicated in plaque buildup in blood vessels, which can lead to health consequences like heart attacks and strokes (McKay, Rogers, and McKay 1989). While we are sometimes reluctant to let go of our anger out of fear that doing so will be interpreted as consent to harmful behavior, it's we who suffer the most immediate effects of our anger. It has been said that being angry at someone is like taking poison and hoping the other person will suffer.

Marcy lives in the realm of separation. She can't escape the trap of feeling that everything she does for herself is against others and everything she does for others is against herself. So she loses either way. Her attempts to be kind to herself result in guilt, while her attempts to care for others arouse her anger. In the light of inter-being, we can see this lose-lose situation for the illusion it is. In reality, everything she does for herself is also done for others. In reality, everything she does for others is also for herself. When she takes care of her own happiness and well-being, she can be deeply present to those who depend on her. When she fails to take care of her own happiness, those who depend on her receive her resentment and anger. Acting for others' happiness simultaneously brings her into harmony with the ultimate reality of no separation. And acting in accord with that reality is the source of great happiness. As a precious manifestation of the universe, she can't ignore loving and nurturing herself any more than she can ignore loving and nurturing others. Both are precious manifestations.

The whole cosmos came together to allow you to manifest. The whole cosmos came together to manifest the other person. These are inseparable realities. Any act of kindness affects the whole.

Will I Lose Myself?

Recently a client commented to me that by giving up his anger and cultivating kindness, he felt as though he were losing himself. This sort of fear is often present when people leave duality behind and grow toward greater peace and happiness. From a Buddhist perspective, we can see that this is one of the traps of thinking in terms of a separate, unchanging self: "I had a lot of anger in me yesterday, so if now I have less anger, what am I? Am I still myself?" This can be unsettling.

At the same time, it's exactly the point of no self. Acting from no self means we aren't trapped *today* by how we were *yesterday*. It means we can walk resolutely in the direction of happiness and well-being without getting caught in the past. In fact, this sense of losing ourselves is part of a more general misperception, the misperception that happiness comes through holding on tightly to what we have and are. The truth is, the more we let go, the happier we become. If we let go a little, there will be some happiness. If we let go completely, our happiness will be total.

The worst way to be yourself is to *try* to be yourself. Paradoxically, you are most yourself when you let go of yourself by relaxing into no-self awareness of the present moment. When you think you are being yourself but you are holding on to past patterns of thinking and behaving, you are only allowing your conditioning to push you around. You confuse your conditioning with yourself. But you are more than your conditioning. When you let go of your conditioning and every sense that you have to remain a certain way or that your life must remain a certain way, then you're free. Then you become what you really are and actually always have been.

Consciousness Is One

The garden of consciousness is one garden. You can't draw a line in the ground and divide your garden from the gardens of others. If you allow weeds to grow wildly in your garden, the wind carries their seeds to the gardens of those around you and, in turn, to those around them. If your neighbors allow weeds to grow, their seeds are carried to your garden. The idea that we can separate them is, as you have seen in this book, at the very heart of delusion.

When we do our best to manage the unwholesome seeds in our own gardens, creating conditions that discourage their growth and dissemination, we at the same time help everyone around us. We can observe this every time we are around someone who's suffering in some way. The other person's sadness, anger, or jealousy can easily be transplanted into us. And if we don't maintain our mindfulness, we may become angry and impatient. So if we know how to take care of our negative seeds, we protect others at the same time.

You can do more than just avoid spreading weeds. You can also water positive seeds in the people around you. No one has only positive qualities. All of us have a mixture of flowers and weeds. Learning to focus on other people's good qualities helps you nourish those qualities in them. This also creates a more whole and nurturing environment around you. And that environment will nourish positive qualities in you as well, creating positive feedback loops of kindness and well-being.

Practice:
Metta Meditation

One of the most rewarding practices you can do, metta meditation, is the intentional cultivation of love and compassion. Begin with yourself first, and then spread kindness to your loved ones, people you feel neutral about, people you find difficult, and finally all beings. The core of this practice is to dwell with kind intentions; for example, "May I be happy" or "May you be happy." However, for this practice to be effective and transformative, the key is finding a way to generate a heartfelt quality. It's unlikely that the mechanical repetition of phrases will be very transformative or help us weaken the illusion of separateness. What's needed is a way to make these intentions vivid and alive.

One way to do this is to spend a few moments summoning up a general sense of yourself as you begin your meditation. Get a feel of your basic goodness in a global way, a sense of your positive intentions throughout your life, your general desire to be a good person and to act in positive, loving ways. Let yourself become aware of what an amazing being you are, how much you have grown, and all you have accomplished.

Then raise a global sense of the difficulties you have faced, using this to open your heart of compassion toward yourself in light of all you have endured and suffered. Most of us have endured quite a bit, and our hearts can easily learn to open to ourselves as we contemplate these difficulties.

Once you have raised a strong feeling of kindness, friendliness, appreciation, and compassion for yourself, let your body and mind rest, bathing them in the warmth and radiance of this feeling. If ideas of your mistakes or imperfections come up, or if you find yourself deciding on ways you need to change, just notice this and let it be. Let the radiance and kindness penetrate every cell of your body, every corner of your consciousness.

You begin with kindness toward self because it's assumed that this is relatively easy to do. For some people, however, this assumption doesn't hold. If that's the case for you, a first step might be to write down what's good about you, along with what you have suffered and endured, breathing in and out while contemplating your list. Should you have difficulty finding positive things about yourself, ask someone you trust to help.

If it's still difficult for you to summon love and compassion for yourself, you might begin with any being you find easy to love. For some people, it could be a child, a loved one who has died, or a pet. Start wherever is easiest, and then bring the feelings of kindness from there over to yourself.

Once you have found a way to generate a strong sense of kindness and compassion toward yourself, then breathe in and out with phrases like these:

- May I have *happiness* and the causes of happiness.

- May I be *safe*, free from harm, illness, and injury.

- May I have *ease* of well-being.

- May I be *free* of afflictive emotions, such as sadness, anger, self-doubt, and envy.

- May I always treat myself with kindness and *understanding*.

- May I become an *enlightened* person, free from sorrow.

After the first few times you work with a given phrase, just use the emphasized word, breathing in and out and holding it in awareness, returning to the full form when your concentration fades. If you find yourself entering a wordless state of love and compassion, stay with that. Let go of the words. And again, if concentration fades, return to the full phrase.

Once you have practiced kindness toward yourself, then summon up a global sense of the goodness and sorrows of a loved one, and continue in the same way: "May he have happiness and the causes of happiness" and so on. Then go on to a neutral person, someone you don't know very well and have no particular positive or negative reaction to. Then continue with someone you have difficulty with and, finally, all beings.

You don't have to do all this in one sitting. Often, you may spend the time on just yourself, on just someone else, or on first yourself and then one other person. Given the inter-being nature of the cosmos, no level of this practice is better than any other.

If you feel stuck or the practice seems dry, don't push. Back off for a time and return another day, rather than force yourself to do what you aren't ready for. What's hard one day may be easy the next.

chapter 6

Taking Care of Our Sorrow

Brothers, why do I call this path the right path? I call it the right path because it does not avoid or deny suffering, but allows for a direct confrontation with suffering as the means to overcome it.

—Buddha

It's useless to pretend that life doesn't contain difficulties, losses, and disappointments. Any path that speaks to us of happiness must also address our unhappiness, our sorrow and suffering. Yes, happiness is always available. We can always find positive elements in the here and now. But sometimes there are painful difficulties as well, and they must not be ignored. Shallow approaches that deny our suffering only leave us frustrated in the end.

The relationship between our sorrow and our happiness is deep. Hunger teaches us the value of having food to eat. Thirst teaches us the value of having water to drink. Losing someone we love shows us the importance of the people still present in our lives. Loss teaches us the value of what we still have.

Our pain teaches us to be empathic and care about others. We don't automatically start out that way. Young children can be astoundingly lacking in empathy, in part because the brain is still developing and also because they lack experience. Until you have been the one who's ostracized by others, you don't really know what that feels like. But once you've had that experience, the possibility opens up for you to learn to empathize with those who suffer rejection and other troubles. All the difficulties of childhood, such as being chosen last for the sports team, failing tests both academic and social, or drawing unwanted attention by being different in some embarrassing way (and young people experience almost all ways of being different as embarrassing), prepare us to become kinder human beings, capable of understanding and compassion. Without such difficulties, including those we face in our adult lives, our capacity for caring and understanding is stillborn, and can't become a fully embodied, living reality.

When the Buddha became enlightened and offered his first teaching, he not only didn't ignore suffering but also, in fact, based his whole approach to happiness and well-being on coming to terms with it. Indeed, it was suffering that propelled the Buddha on his spiritual quest in the first place. In the traditional legend, encounters with an old person, a sick person, and a dead person launched the pampered young prince Siddhattha into a profound existential crisis. To this intelligent and sensitive young person, these were devastating realities. They disturbed him so much he couldn't continue to ignore them by resting comfortably in the luxuries of his palace. He had to understand them and find the path of release, both for himself and for others.

It's natural for us to want to be happy and avoid suffering. Because of this, we employ psychological defenses to deny life's realities. The Buddha's strategy is different. The Buddha's strategy is to look *right at* our suffering. He knew that, rather than ignore our suffering, we in fact need to do the opposite: respect it, remain open to it, contemplate it, and even befriend it. Looking deeply at our suffering reveals the path of nonsuffering. Only when we do this can we find the way to true happiness.

Without the reality of suffering, enlightenment would be impossible. True happiness would be impossible. Looking honestly at our suffering without distorting or defending, but instead applying wisdom and patience, is the source of the energy of enlightenment itself. Our sorrow motivates us to look deeply into our human predicament. When we come to see how thoroughly we're caught in the net of suffering, we have the right kind of energy to see the path out of it.

The First Noble Truth: Understanding Dukkha

The Buddhist term for suffering is *dukkha*. Dukkha can be translated as "pain," "sorrow," "suffering," or "misery." It also means "imperfection." Even very refined mental states cultivated in meditation are considered dukkha, because while valuable, they fail to provide ultimate release. Practitioners who reach the highest levels of meditation are still caught in dukkha, since the moment they stop meditating, dukkha is once again apparent.

Dukkha also means "emptiness" (*śūnyatā*). Emptiness means lacking a separate, inherently existing self. More broadly, dukkha signifies the basic unsatisfactoriness of things. In other words, dukkha is a very comprehensive term. It includes not only being diagnosed with a terminal illness but also being unable to find a parking place. It includes major problems as well as the hangnails of life. With such a rich cluster of meanings, it's sometimes best to use the word "dukkha" itself rather than translate it.

The insight of dukkha was so important to the Buddha that he made it the cornerstone of his teaching. In his first sermon, he taught what he called the four noble truths, the first of which is dukkha. In his later years, after giving many teachings to many different kinds of people, he emphasized that all he ever taught was dukkha and how to bring it to an end. He considered it that important.

Dukkha, the hard fact of human suffering, is a noble truth, a sacred truth. Dukkha is the foundation of Buddhist teaching. To fully understand the truth of dukkha is the equivalent of complete enlightenment. When we understand dukkha, our misery comes to an end. Only happiness and peace remain.

Here's how the Buddha himself described dukkha in his first teaching:

> Birth is dukkha, aging is dukkha, sickness is dukkha, death is dukkha; sorrow and lamentation, pain, grief, and despair are dukkha; association with the unpleasant is dukkha; dissociation from the pleasant is dukkha; not to get what one wants is dukkha—in brief, the five aggregates of attachment are dukkha (Dhammacakkappavattana-sutta; in Rahula 1974, 93).

Though we readily recognize most of the items on this list as painful, we might not immediately think of birth as suffering. From a Buddhist point of view, birth is suffering in two ways: First and most immediate, just listen to the cry of the child being born, ripped from the safety of the womb and feeling the pain and separateness of the world! We may be happy because there's new life, but when we listen, we also hear the sound of dukkha.

Yet the birth process is only the beginning. For birth is the start of the many difficulties we face in life, the many dashed hopes, painful relationships, and everything else on the Buddha's list—sickness, death, and all the rest. And that's the second sense in which birth is considered dukkha. Birth is dukkha in the sense that it's the beginning of all our troubles.

The last item on the Buddha's list also requires a word of explanation. He says the five aggregates of form, feeling, perception, mental formations, and consciousness are also dukkha. These aren't automatically dukkha but become so because of our *attachment* to them as a self, as "me" or "mine." It's because of this attachment that our mental and physical continuum brings us a lot of sorrow as we experience unpleasant sensations and thoughts, as we get sick, grow old, and die.

A Realistic View

The way to freedom, peace, and love begins with looking deeply into our suffering. This isn't pessimistic; it's realistic. The judgment that Buddhism is pessimistic stems from the denial of dukkha that's prevalent in our culture. We put sick people away in hospitals. We put old people away in nursing homes. We send dead people to funeral homes. Even our religious and spiritual beliefs in an afterlife or in reincarnation can function as a defense against the reality of death and the difficulties of life. This only seems pessimistic in the context of our cultural tendency to hide from painful realities.

Visiting Europe's great cathedrals and museums, you encounter a lot of religious art that depicts the sufferings of Christ and the saints. It can almost seem that religion in the West makes a fetish of suffering and pain, which is in stark contrast to the many images of peaceful Buddhas and bodhisattvas in the East. It would be nice if, as some have argued, we had more depictions of a peaceful and happy Jesus, of peaceful and happy saints, radiant with the peace and love of their connection with the divine. At the same time, however, an unexamined rejection of the suffering of Christ and the saints betrays our cultural denial of life's difficulties and the reality of death. Though they can reflect an

149

unwholesome fascination with the terrible, all these depictions of suffering are offered in a context of transcendent meaning, and ultimately aim at affirming that life is good even though we suffer.

We react strangely when confronted with dukkha. Sometimes when you share your pain with others, they respond in a way that clearly betrays anxiety. This might take the form of platitudes, such as "I'm sure it will turn out for the best," advice to turn our concerns over to God, or even a lecture about being more positive. We act as though dukkha is an anomaly, an unnatural interruption of the perfect, easy, and comfortable life we think we should have. So when dukkha manifests, it must be someone's fault. We can even blame the very people who are suffering for bringing it on themselves by not thinking positively, by being too negative. And when someone dies, we act as though this is a completely unexpected and unnatural event. We want to blame someone: the doctor, the hospital—anyone at hand will do.

But dukkha is not an anomaly. It's part of life. When we can accept the reality of dukkha, we can relax. We don't have to distort our consciousness by using defense mechanisms. We can see life whole, entire, as it is. For we can never really affirm life if we don't acknowledge the whole truth.

When you tell your sorrows to someone who understands that dukkha is a natural part of life, it can be a great relief. They offer no platitudes. They don't try to explain it away. They don't blame or distort. They simply are present with you in silent awe before the sacred truth of human sorrow. To be able to speak the truth is already a relief. It's a relief not to have to pretend.

Looking Deeply into Dukkha

If you fall and break your leg, everyone can see that this is dukkha. If you are laid off from work and have a lot of financial worries, everyone can see this is dukkha. If you have a major health problem, lose someone you love, or even get a speeding ticket, we can all see that this is dukkha. But this obvious kind of suffering isn't the whole story.

At a deeper level, dukkha is based on impermanence. At this level, even things we normally consider to be positive are marked with dukkha because of their temporary nature. You may feel very happy when you fall in love, but this ignores how relationships change and eventually, one way or another, come to an end. The less prepared you are for this, the more the wonder of falling in love will come to cause you pain. Buying a wonderful new car may give you pleasure, but when someone dings the side panel with a car door in a parking lot, your pleasure turns to sorrow. The wonderful new puppy you bring home all too quickly becomes an elderly, arthritic animal that needs a lot of care, costing a lot of money in vet bills, though that pales compared with the heartache.

Everything that manifests, everything we experience, is the result of complex causes and conditions coming together, factors reaching far beyond the thing itself. New love is the result of many complicated factors of attraction and psychological preparedness coming together at the right time and with the right person. The new car is the result of many factors, including your financial capacity to pay for it, the work of many people at the factory, the people at the car dealership, and so on. The puppy is the result of a mother dog and a father dog, and their whole genetic ancestry, combined with a breeder or someone who cares for the newborn and makes it available to you. But anything that's dependent on so many external factors is also subject to change when those factors change. And change they will. If enough of those factors change, the object of your pleasure is no longer manifest. Love turns to hatred. The beautiful car becomes scrap. The dog dies. And because we don't fully acknowledge and accept impermanence, we suffer greatly.

There's another option. If you know deeply that everything is impermanent, if you see this clearly and with wisdom, then you won't cling so tightly even to the people and things that give you joy. To fully understand impermanence allows you to enjoy everything without clinging in desperation. Only in this way is it safe to enjoy the good things of life. In fact, true enjoyment of the beautiful things in life is only possible if you know impermanence. Otherwise, a subtle fear creeps in along with our pleasure—the fear of losing what we love. If you cling, if you don't recognize the impermanent nature of everything, then suffering results. The more you can accept with serenity that everything that has a beginning also has an ending, the more freedom and joy you will have.

Even when we practice mindfulness, clinging creeps in subtly. We can learn to be in the present moment, breathe and smile, and enjoy the blue sky. But if the next day is cloudy, we feel disappointed. Our disappointment reveals that another element was at work when we looked at the sky, not merely simple, mindful enjoyment—an element of clinging. There was an element of discrimination in our enjoyment of the blue sky: We liked the blue sky, and all we wanted were blue skies. We didn't want cloudy skies. Our sadness is not caused by the cloudy sky, but by our clinging to blue skies, to our notion that the sky should always be blue.

And there's a deeper level of suffering called "pervasive suffering." Everything is full of suffering as long as we remain unenlightened. We can catch glimpses of this if we are attentive. While doing chores in the yard, we're already planning what we'll do next. In this way, there's always a subtle feeling that we can't be happy *now*. The suffering involved here is subtle, but because of it, we find little intrinsic pleasure in *doing* our yard work. We only find pleasure in its *being done*. And even that pleasure doesn't last long. For very quickly, we turn our attention to whatever is next, and experience that in the same way: we're not happy until there's completion and, even then, not fully happy since something always remains incomplete.

Awareness of Dukkha Helps

Whenever we catch a glimpse of dukkha, we should let ourselves see it as clearly as possible rather than run from it. For the awareness of dukkha creates the energy to become an enlightened person. Sorrow motivates the search for peace.

Acknowledging the truth of dukkha lets our awareness be clear, open, and undistorted. When we try to deny painful realities, we use a lot of psychic energy that could be directed toward our happiness and freedom, toward enlightenment. Denial of reality ends up hurting us. However much I deny that there's a wall in front of me, trying to walk through it will still hurt.

When we look deeply into our suffering, we see the way out. But how will we see it if we pretend it doesn't exist? Working with dukkha is like walking south by keeping the North Star at our backs. Seeing the workings of dukkha allows us to walk in the direction of happiness. Denying dukkha complicates our neurotic misery.

—————— Practice: ——————
"This Is Dukkha"

Awareness of dukkha can't help us if it remains abstract or theoretical. But if we can connect this teaching with our daily lives, it has the power to liberate us.

As you go through daily life, recognize dukkha whenever it arises. Don't deny it. Can you feel the presence of dukkha when you are late and rushing to work? Can you feel dukkha as anxiety arises in you about an important meeting? Can you feel the dukkha of impatience as you stand in a long line at the market? Can you let yourself know the subtle dukkha of just being scattered, thinking ahead too much and not being in the present moment?

Whenever dukkha arises, tell yourself clearly, "This is dukkha." Let yourself experience the relief of simply acknowledging the truth.

The Second Noble Truth: Suffering Has a Cause (*Samudaya*)

A man comes home to a bare apartment. All the furniture is gone. On the counter is a note scrawled in the distinctive hand of his wife. It reads simply, "I'm leaving you." No reason. No way to contact her. No discussion. Just the bare apartment and these three words.

Such situations happen. And when they do, we are in the realm of dukkha. This is suffering in one of its most bare and obvious forms.

If we try to look into the cause of this man's suffering, we can imagine many factors that may have been at work. Perhaps he'd been an unkind husband, and his wife had finally had enough. Perhaps she's someone who needs change and excitement more than a stable relationship. Maybe she fell in love with someone else. Maybe she is gay and can no longer tolerate the safe pretense of a straight marriage. Maybe some element of the relationship deteriorated, the sexual element or the friendship element. Maybe financial pressures finally got the best of this relationship. There are many possible factors.

But what if we look still more deeply, if we look into this man's miserable situation with the eyes of the Buddha? At the deepest level, what's the cause of his present sorrow?

154

The insight of the Buddha is that the cause of sorrow here lies ultimately with what he called *taṇhā*, meaning "thirst," or "craving." Some of the previous factors may have been at work, but the deep cause is really this craving, this clinging and attachment. Without the tendency to cling, there would be no suffering.

The point certainly isn't to blame this man for desiring his wife. We sympathize with someone in such a situation. It's not a matter of blame. It's a matter of cause and effect. Where thirst or craving is present, when it attaches to things that are impermanent in their actual nature and don't have a separate, inherent self, to things that are the result of many complex factors coming together, suffering is the result. Not sometimes. Always. Not just for some of us. For all of us. For how many of us will lose the ones we love most in the world? Every one of us will, whether through our own or our partner's death, or through divorce or the end of the relationship. How many of us will ultimately be separated from what we love the most? None of us is immune to this. But if you remove the element of attachment, you remove the suffering.

Removing craving doesn't mean we become indifferent. By giving up clinging, we can enjoy the good things in our lives even more. We enjoy them more because fear of loss is no longer present. We can be deeply glad for our spouse or partner's presence in our lives. Knowing that this type of presence is impermanent invites us to cherish it more deeply, without taking it for granted.

If someone is rendered homeless from gambling debts or dies from a heroin overdose, if someone gambles recklessly on the stock market and loses it all, we can easily see that such suffering was the result of craving. But the Buddha's teaching about craving includes subtler forms of clinging that most of us would accept as normal, like attachment to a partner. Sometimes these subtle, normal forms are even more pernicious because they're harder to see. But the same principle is at work.

Looking Deeper: The Nature of Craving

Buddhist scriptures were handed down orally for generations before being written down. To aid oral transmission, sometimes one term would be used to stand for a longer list of things. So craving could be considered the first element in a list that includes other unwholesome mental states, such as those cited in the Parable of the Cloth Sutra: enmity, anger, rancor, hypocrisy, malice, jealousy, avarice, trickery, deceit, obduracy, haughtiness, pride, arrogance, inflation, and indolence (Rahula 1974). These unskillful mental states are also sources of our sorrow.

We can also understand dukkha as stemming from the three poisons: craving, ignorance, and aversion. And at the root of these three is ignorance (*avidyā*), or lack of wisdom. It's lack of wisdom that makes us cling to some things and reject others, rather than recognize that their selfless and impermanent nature makes such reactions pointless and ultimately painful. Seeking the things we crave and avoiding the things we dislike launches us into a perpetual and futile struggle, preventing us from resting open and aware in the present moment. Our craving and aversion are what set up afflictive emotional states.

The philosopher-emperor Marcus Aurelius expressed this in a striking image: "The sphere of the soul maintains its perfect form," he wrote, "when it is not extended toward any object or shrinking in on itself, or dispersed or sunk down, but only when it is bathed in light. The light in which it sees the truth, both in all things and in itself" (Forstater 2000, 162–63). The soul that loses its roundness or wholeness by extending toward an object is an image of craving. "Shrinking in on itself" expresses aversion, a pulling back from unpleasantness. Being whole, round, undistorted, or bathed in light depicts a consciousness that's mindful and undistorted by the ignorance of desire or aversion.

Craving manifests subtly in the everyday itch for entertainment, the underlying restlessness and lack of contentment. It's any state that prevents us from being content and happy in the present moment and the present circumstance.

Understanding dukkha isn't about trying to get all of this straight philosophically. It's about seeing for yourself, very clearly, how this works. Our lack of wisdom, acting as if things are separate and permanent, sets up craving and aversion, and all the unwholesome mental states. If we see this repeatedly and deeply, we can end the vicious cycle of suffering Buddhists call *samsāra*.

To this point the Buddha has functioned in his role as "medicine king," identifying the illness and explaining its etiology. The illness is dukkha. It's caused by craving, aversion, and ignorance. Eliminating the cause leads to the cure.

Practice:
Noting Craving and Aversion

We have a tendency to only see dukkha when it manifests in one of its most powerful forms, such as in the case of the man abandoned by his wife. In the practice for the first noble truth, you had the opportunity to see it less abstractly and more immediately, perhaps even catching a glimpse of the pervasiveness of dukkha. Similarly, in this practice you have the opportunity to experience craving and aversion (and their underlying cause, ignorance) in a simple and direct way. With this practice, you can get a little better acquainted with your own mind and how it spins out dukkha from moment to moment.

To do this practice, sit comfortably upright and let yourself enjoy your inbreath and your outbreath. Whenever a thought pulls you away from the sensations of breathing, notice the thought that has pulled you away and ask yourself, What is its nature? Does it contain the element of craving or desire? Is there a feeling of wanting this or avoiding that? Is there a sense that things have to go a certain way (desire)? Or does it contain aversion, a feeling that things must *not* go a certain way? Does it contain a mixture of both? Observe each thought to notice what you are hoping to have and what you are hoping to avoid.

The Third Noble Truth: Suffering Can Be Stopped (*Nirodha*)

If these insights are to free us, we have to work with them to make them part of us, part of how we look at the world. When that begins to happen, freedom and happiness arise spontaneously. When suffering is removed, happiness and well-being shine forth.

The good news of Buddhism is contained in this third noble truth: suffering can be stopped. To accomplish this, we need to see the nature of reality with depth and clarity. It's like when someone sticks a knife into a toaster to try to retrieve a piece of bread that got stuck and is starting to burn. She may have an intellectual understanding that this is a bad idea, but once she experiences the actual electrical shock from doing it, her understanding is no longer just intellectual. After that, she doesn't need anyone to tell her that sticking a knife in the toaster is a bad idea. She doesn't have to struggle with herself to avoid it. She *knows*. It's this kind of knowing—the knowing of *effective insight*—that's needed if we are to leave suffering behind.

You can come to know this truth deeply by noticing dukkha when it arises, but you can also come to a deep knowing of the truth of cessation from the positive side. When you are quiet and content, when there's no itch to get up and do or find entertainment or diversion, when you are just present, there's a profound happiness, peace, and contentment. What makes this experience so pleasant? It's precisely because in such a moment, neither desire nor aversion pushes or pulls at us. We simply are. Our consciousness is balanced and harmonious. Such experiences may be brief and far between, but we can learn to notice, extend, and multiply them.

It may be difficult for us to fully understand how suffering can come to an end, but we don't have to take this on blind faith either. After only a little bit of training, all of us can begin to experience this to some extent. When we learn to ease up even a little on our likes and dislikes, we can begin to experience more spaciousness, greater peace and happiness. When we feel that, though we'd *prefer* things go a certain way, it's okay if they go differently, we already begin to experience greater ease of well-being. This much we can easily come to see for ourselves.

How do we stop craving and thereby stop dukkha? We don't have to struggle against our craving. Remember, struggle perpetuates the problem. It's enough to be mindful, to notice what's going on and let it be, releasing not only our craving and aversion but also our opinions, beliefs, and views, so we can gradually learn to be present to the underlying happiness that's there waiting for us.

Even when we have eliminated all inordinate craving and attachment, sadness and other emotions may still arise in our consciousness. This doesn't necessarily mean suffering is present. To become a Buddha doesn't mean to become insensate, like a hunk of metal. Becoming a Buddha is the fulfillment of our human nature, not its destruction. So if sadness arises and we let ourselves know the sadness without repressing it, then we can see that this mental state is impermanent and selfless. As such, it passes through us unimpeded. It's when we add resistance and struggle that suffering enters in. When we say to ourselves, "I feel sad, and this is awful! This is terrible! This must not be so! I must only have happy feelings at all times," suffering is present. A perfect Buddha wouldn't necessarily see the arising of sadness as problematic, as long as she doesn't resist the experience, and instead allows it to flow naturally.

Sometimes an image helps us understand. To envision cessation of suffering, think of the Buddha sitting peacefully with his begging bowl in front of him. Sometimes wonderful things are placed in his bowl. Sometimes terrible things come. But since he has ceased to identify with the push-pull of desire and aversion, he remains undisturbed either way. His mind doesn't become agitated or distressed. He can be present and happy with whatever shows up.

—— Practice: ——
Notice Cessation of Suffering

To understand the truth of the cessation of suffering, it helps to notice that this is a state that's already familiar to some extent. Perhaps you'll catch yourself, even briefly, feeling happy and peaceful in a moment of contentment, not rushing toward the future or ruminating about the past, not wishing anything to be different. Whenever that experience arises spontaneously, pause. Notice. Allow yourself to enjoy it.

Also, when you notice craving or aversion, you'll note that sometimes just by noticing what's going on, just by noticing that that's what you're experiencing, the mind already releases this tendency, and a moment of peace opens up in you. Of course, major life problems and difficulties won't dissolve easily, but require gentle persistence to release. But with less difficult things, you can sometimes experience the tension of craving and aversion releasing simply by noticing. This is a taste of enlightenment. Be alert for it.

The Fourth Noble Truth: The Path (*Marga*)

It's natural for us to ask what, specifically, we should do to free ourselves from suffering. Answers won't always be to our liking, however, for to deluded mind, freedom looks like slavery, and unhappiness masquerades as happiness. It might seem as if freeing ourselves demands a lot of sacrifice and pain, a lot of giving up of things we enjoy. But this is a trick of deluded mind.

In a sense, the path to liberation is very simple. One time, a man who was the student of another teacher asked the Buddha how his disciples practiced. The Buddha told him that his disciples walked, sat, ate, and rested. The man became confused. He told the Buddha that he and his fellow students did these things as well. The Buddha pointed out that there was a difference, however. For when his disciples walked, they knew they were walking. When they sat, they knew they were sitting. When they ate, they knew they were eating. And when they rested, they knew they were resting.

In other words, to return to the present moment, to know what's going on inside you and around you, is already enlightenment and, at the same time, the practice of enlightenment. When you can be present with what's happening now, you're not preoccupied with your worries and hopes, your craving and aversion.

At the same time the Buddha taught the four noble truths, he also taught the middle way. The way to enlightenment is to follow the middle path between the extremes of dedication to sensory pleasure, on the one hand, and to strictness, to harsh asceticism and mortification, on the other. Both of these, the Buddha taught, are pointless. Both are dukkha.

In our cultural context, a harsh asceticism isn't generally our problem. What's difficult for us to understand is that the unrestrained pursuit of pleasure is destructive. We tend to equate

161

pleasure with happiness, so we are much more likely to get stuck on the pleasure-seeking side of the dilemma. But it isn't really hard to see that everything pleasant isn't necessarily good for us, but can instead cause future suffering.

For those who want specific information about how to become liberated, the Buddha offered the fourth noble truth, the noble eightfold path. The noble eightfold path is the way of living that leads in the direction of enlightenment and true happiness. The eight items on this list are:

- Right view

- Right thought

- Right speech

- Right action

- Right livelihood

- Right diligence

- Right mindfulness

- Right concentration

Let's take a look at what the Buddha meant by these.

The first thing to notice is that the Buddha isn't prescribing arbitrary, moralistic rules here. For this reason, the term translated as "right" (*samyak*) is best understood as meaning something like wholesome, beneficial, leading away from suffering, or conducive to well-being. If you want to be free from dukkha, the Buddha recommends these eight practices as being especially valuable, for these practices line us up with the true, nirvana nature of reality. They can be grouped into three aspects: wisdom practices, behavioral practices, and mental training.

Wisdom Practices

Right view and right thinking constitute the wisdom elements of the eightfold path. To see things correctly, to think in accord with how things really are, means to recognize the no-self and impermanent nature of everything you see. The full practice of wisdom here is, once again, not merely intellectual knowing, but penetrating insight. To see everything as impermanent and nonself means to look at everything as a full manifestation of the cosmos, not just a separate object. We see that the flower contains the rain, the soil, the sunshine, and ultimately everything else as well. To practice right view and right thinking means to look at everything in this light. When everything is seen in this light, the natural consequence is love and compassion.

Right thinking also means right intention. It's our intention that generates positive or negative karma. If we accidentally cause harm, we don't necessarily accrue bad karma. Further, practicing with the clear intention to benefit others and ourselves gives us the energy we need to practice deeply and with commitment.

Behavioral Practices

The way we are living now grows out of deluded, unenlightened mind. This path continues to hold out false hope, while always disappointing us in the end, leading us deeper and deeper into dukkha. It simply stands to reason that we won't get a radical shift of insight while continuing to live in the same way.

The behavioral changes proposed by the Buddha are right speech, right action, and right livelihood. Right speech contains the elements of both truthfulness and kindness. Right speech also involves refraining from gossip, from passing on information that we don't know for sure is true or that can cause divisions in our community. It also involves refraining from conversation that's trivial or meaningless. This doesn't mean that all conversation must be intellectual. To tell someone during a shared meal that the food is delicious or to point out a beautiful tree can be right speech, since it invites the listener back to the present moment.

Right action is action that does no harm, action that's beneficial and kind. Acting unkindly obstructs awareness of the interconnectedness of things and strengthens the illusion of separateness, isolation, and alienation. Right action is based on the perception of interconnectedness, the insight that what we normally see as being outside of ourselves is actually still ourselves, since the terms "inside" and "outside" have no ultimate reality.

Right livelihood means to make your living, to the extent possible, in ways that don't harm others. The classic examples in the Buddhist texts are to refrain from manufacturing weapons or intoxicants, or butchering animals. These examples are relatively clear, but beyond them, practicing right livelihood quickly gets into more of a gray area. If you earn your living selling ice cream, that may, at first blush, seem innocent enough. But in a culture suffering many health problems related to obesity, this isn't as innocent as it seems. Once again, the point is to try to line up your behavior in daily life with the insight of interbeing, of loving-kindness. None of us may have work that's solely beneficial, but we can do our best to go in the right direction.

Mental Training

Mental training includes the elements of right diligence, right mindfulness, and right concentration.

Right diligence means cultivating wholesome mental states. We learn to water the positive elements in our consciousness, elements such as kindness, happiness, and peace, while not encouraging the elements rooted in separation and delusion, such as anger and envy. These issues will be familiar to you from chapter 4.

One gardening strategy is to fill all the available space with plants you want to have, thus preventing weeds from gaining a foothold. In the same way, assiduously encouraging wholesome mental states in your consciousness allows less room for other kinds of states to manifest. At the same time, of course, some unwholesome states will continue to manifest. When this happens, we use the approach of mindful embracing, as previously described.

Right mindfulness means to be aware of what's going on in the present moment. Mindful attention nourishes the lovely plants in the garden of our consciousness, stimulating them to grow and flourish. It also naturally discourages unwholesome mental states, making it more difficult for them to manifest and causing them to manifest for shorter periods of time when they do arise.

Closely linked to mindfulness is right concentration. Mindfulness is like a floodlight of attention. It illuminates what's going on with a wide beam, showing many things at once. Concentration is like a laser beam. When you are mindful, you are aware of things going on around you and inside you. Perhaps you notice, among these many things, a beautiful cloud. So you stop and breathe in and out, and focus all of your attention on the cloud. If you do this deeply, the sense that you and the cloud are separate fades away. You sense a deep connectedness. You know that both you and the cloud are water. When you do this, you have shifted from mindfulness to concentration. But both involve the exercise of clear awareness, uncontaminated by our fears and preoccupations.

The Centrality of Mindfulness

A wonderful Jewish legend goes something like this: Whenever the people were in trouble, the rabbi would go to a secret, holy place deep in the woods. There he would light the sacred fire and say the sacred prayer, and God would hear. The danger would be averted. As the generations passed, people no longer knew where the sacred place was. But they remembered the sacred fire and the sacred prayer. And it was enough. When difficulties arose, the prayers were heard, and the danger was averted. Still later, no one knew how to light the sacred fire anymore, but even just remembering the sacred prayer was enough. Finally, a time came when no one knew the sacred place or how to light the sacred fire, or even the words of the sacred prayer. But they remembered that there once had been a sacred place, a sacred fire, and a sacred prayer. And their remembering was enough.

Mindfulness is enough. Mindfulness connects to all the other elements. At the same time, to be mindful is to practice right view and right thinking. You begin to grasp that you aren't separate from everyone and everything else. If you are mindful, you are aware of what you say and how it affects yourself and others, so you are practicing right speech. If you are mindful, you are aware of the effects of your actions and of how you earn your living. So you are already beginning to practice right action and right livelihood. In the same way, mindfulness leads you into the practice of right diligence and right concentration. So when you feel confused, just remember to come back to yourself—to your breathing, your body, and your consciousness—practicing being aware of what's happening. As your perceptions gradually clear and deepen, you will find your way through every difficulty. As long as you maintain mindfulness, it will be all right.

So how do we gradually learn to reduce the inordinate craving that's responsible for so much of our sorrow? Be mindful. Be in touch with your suffering. Know it *as* suffering. See its roots, its causes. When you see the roots, you, at the same time, begin to know the way out of the trap of dukkha. Also be in touch with what's healing and refreshing. These elements can heal our sorrow if we make deep enough contact with them.

A Treasury of Insight

One day the Buddha stood silently before 1,250 monks and nuns, holding up a flower. He just stood there saying nothing at all as the moments passed. Finally, a monk named Mahakashyapa smiled at the Buddha. Mahakashyapa understood. And the Buddha saw that he understood, and smiled back at him. The Buddha said, "I have a treasure of insight, and I have transmitted it to Mahakashyapa."

What was it that Mahakashyapa understood? Perhaps he understood that the flower was already teaching the dharma more powerfully than any words the Buddha could use. The flower was silently teaching impermanence, for while it was a flower that day, it would soon wilt, fade, and be tossed on the garbage heap. The flower was silently teaching no self, revealing itself not as something separate, but as a complete manifestation of the cosmos. The flower was teaching the four noble truths, showing that all our suffering is the result of struggling to grasp what can't be grasped, since it's always changing and never a separately existing thing to begin with.

But to say all this is still a little too linear, too cerebral. More simply, the point is to *see the flower*. When you touch the flower with your mindfulness, you know what a precious manifestation it is, made only more precious by its temporariness and by its miraculous interconnectedness with everything else. Seeing it this way, you don't need to cling. You don't need to try to freeze the flower in time, coat it with plastic, take a photograph, or press it between the pages of a book. It's enough to enjoy it in the present moment.

When you can do that, you have moved beyond dukkha. Then the smile of Mahakashyapa will bloom on your own lips.

chapter 7

Practicing Happiness

He who has realized the Truth, Nirvana, is the happiest being in the world. He is free from all "complexes" and obsessions, the worries and trouble that torment others. His mental health is perfect. He does not repeat the past, nor does he brood over the future. He lives fully in the present moment.

—Walpola Rahula

This chapter addresses the aspect of the eightfold path that's concerned with mental training. It offers a number of meditation practices for you to enjoy.

Of central importance is the attitude with which you go about these practices. Please remember that means and ends can't be separated: you can't go about practicing in a harsh or severe way, and end up creating peace and joy. Harshness and severity only yield more harshness and severity. Going about practice with a sense that you must suffer today to feel happy tomorrow isn't the best way. You must meditate in a way that expresses the peace and joy already within you. That way your practice will deepen quickly and easily.

No less an authority than Zen master Thich Nhat Hanh (2009, 70) emphasizes this point quite clearly: "The practice should be enjoyable and pleasant," he writes. "The elements called joy and pleasure, *mudita* and *priti* in Sanskrit, are a very important part of meditation. If you suffer during meditation, your practice is not correct. Practice should be enjoyable and pleasant. It should be full of joy."

If we can say there's an element of diligence in the practice, it's just enough to let you stretch a little, not so much that it causes you a lot of pain or distress, or tempts you to give up. Just as how, when exercising to improve your health, you should feel refreshed afterward—perhaps pleasantly tired but by no means extremely fatigued or exhausted—so you shouldn't push too hard in meditation either. You meditate in a way that helps you learn to appreciate it, to value it and enjoy it, so you would miss it if you were forced to abandon it. The Buddha's insight of the middle way instructs us that practice is about working *with* our nature, not against it. And when we cross that line, things become unnecessarily difficult. At that point, we've infected our meditation with the same impatient, goal-oriented emphasis we have toward the rest of life, leaving it full of tension and striving.

This point is easily misunderstood. There's a tendency, even in Buddhist circles, to focus on discipline and miss the joy of practice. But I find again and again that when I approach practice in a peaceful, open, and relaxed way, it goes much better and much deeper than when I have a forced, clenched-teeth kind of attitude toward it. Forgetting this causes unnecessary frustration.

One reason for this misunderstanding is that it may sound like forcing yourself to feel peaceful and happy. Of course, that won't work. The practice is never about forcing, including forcing positive states. However, when you approach practice in the right spirit, peaceful and happy feelings tend to arise from simply being open and present. They're by-products of being present and mindful. When thoughts and feelings of sadness, worry, guilt, regret, envy, or other painful mental states arise, if we don't resist them, but remain open and present, they ultimately resolve into more positive mental states. Painful states contain the energy of enlightenment itself, and only need to be touched with our mindfulness to be transformed.

When I teach, I am frequently asked how to find the discipline to meditate regularly. I always find this question a little difficult to respond to. For me, it isn't a matter of discipline. I wouldn't want to leave the house in the morning without having meditated any more than I would want to leave without brushing my teeth or putting on clothes. I enjoy doing the practice, and it prepares me for facing the difficulties of life.

Just as the Buddha spoke of his practice as nonpractice, we could say the discipline is nondiscipline. Eighth-century Zen master Ma-tsu must have had this in mind when he taught, "The Tao [the underlying principle of harmony] has nothing to do with discipline" (Watts 1957, 97; bracketed text added). It has nothing to do with discipline in the sense that, if it were a matter of disclipline, then the Tao could be lost once discipline were no longer necessary. And yet, there's a kind of effortless effort involved here, causing Ma-tsu to add, "[But] if you say that there is no discipline, this is to be the same as ordinary people..." (ibid.; bracketed text added).

The Buddha teaches us to approach practice as nonpractice. Practice without feeling that you are doing something heroic or difficult, something that gives more bragging rights to the ego. Just practice in a relaxed, happy way, without struggling or striving, without trying to get anything or achieve anything. Practice by opening to the happiness within and around you. Meditation isn't some bitter pill you have to swallow.

Acceptance

If you remember just one thing about how to approach meditation practice, please remember the word "acceptance." Meditation is the practice of acceptance of whatever's actually occurring. Some days your mind is all over the place. Let that be okay. Remember that this is the result of causes and conditions, not a verdict about you. What you often think of as a self, you may recall, is really just these same causes and conditions. Other days, your mind is more peaceful. Let that be okay too, without imagining that this means something special, as though now you are suddenly a great adept. Tomorrow will always be different. Whatever the day brings, let it be okay.

Acceptance can easily be misunderstood. Fundamentally, it means the willingness to experience whatever's going on in the present moment, an orientation of opening to what *is* rather than struggling against it. Obviously, it doesn't mean that what is will always be pleasant or what we would prefer; sometimes it's quite the opposite. Acceptance means not succumbing to the delusion that the universe is fundamentally askew because things aren't going in accord with your wishes. Acceptance doesn't mean that you have to be passive or that you can't act to change an unpleasant situation if possible. It just means that you accept being in the situation where you find yourself. And in the same way, you also accept doing what needs to be done in that situation.

Acceptance means surrendering to what is. It means allowing things to be just as they are, since they will be that way anyway. If your mind is very busy during a meditation period, let it be that way and do your best to be present to it, opening to it rather than closing down on it. If you try to force your mind to be less busy, you set yourself up as over, against, and separate from nature, as though you were a separate self. Acceptance means allowing yourself to be in harmony with what's happening.

You might find it helpful to make a small sign with the word "acceptance" on it. Place it where you can see it during meditation to remind yourself to practice in this spirit.

Practical Concerns

There are a number of practical concerns to consider as you develop a meditation practice. What follows is a brief introduction to them.

Posture and Position

You can meditate in four basic positions: lying, sitting, standing, or walking. All four have value, and this chapter provides examples of each.

When most people think of meditation, they probably picture someone in the classic seated position. There's a reason for this. The seated position is perhaps the fullest expression of alert, calm awareness. Lying down, you might become too relaxed or even fall asleep. Standing or walking may induce a mental attitude that's overly busy or lacking in tranquility. Proper sitting helps entrain the kind of calm, open, accepting awareness that's the heart of meditation.

The lotus position, in which the feet are brought up to rest on the opposite thighs, is the classic meditation position in the East. This position, when mastered, allows for effortless stability. But for most of us in the West, it's painful, if we can manage it at all. The half lotus, in which just one foot is brought to rest on the opposite thigh, is a compromise, though also difficult. In our culture we don't usually sit cross-legged on the floor. We sit in chairs. For this reason, such positions can be difficult and unnatural for most of us.

To sit cross-legged on a meditation cushion or upright in a chair is just fine. Let your posture express an attitude of alert calmness. Sit upright but relaxed, neither rigid nor tense. Trying to eliminate all of the spine's natural curvature to be ramrod straight creates too much stress and tension. If you're sitting on a chair, you might feel the most stable putting your feet flat on the floor to create a sense of solidity.

Ultimately, there are no rules. Since I'm used to sitting on a cushion on the floor, my legs just naturally seem to want to cross, even when I sit in a chair. So just find a posture you can maintain comfortably for the meditation period, one that expresses the mental attitude of being relaxed and awake.

Time and Place

In the Sutra on the Four Foundations of Mindfulness (*Satipatthana Sutta*), we find this description of how to meditate: "He [the meditator] goes to the forest, to the foot of a tree, or to an empty room, sits down cross-legged in the lotus position, holds his body straight, and establishes mindfulness in front of him. He breathes in, aware that he is breathing in. He breathes out, aware that he is breathing out" (Thich Nhat Hanh 1990, 4; bracketed text added).

From this description, we see that it's helpful to find a quiet place, a place of solitude or, at least, one where you won't likely be interrupted. Don't obsess about perfection with regard to quiet, however. Even the most remote mountain cave in Nepal won't be perfectly quiet, but may have the sound of blowing wind or dripping water. So if you live in the city with the sounds of traffic and emergency vehicle sirens, or if you live in the country with the sounds of roosters crowing or dogs barking, let this be and don't struggle against the natural facts of your surroundings (acceptance). Instead let yourself be in harmony with whatever's around you.

In the morning the mind is fresh and clear, and often capable of greater ease of concentration than later in the day, when you're tired. If you're too sleepy in the morning, have a cup of tea or coffee first to help you wake up. This is quite in keeping with traditional practices in the East, especially tea, which is sometimes called the "taste of Zen." Drink your tea or coffee mindfully, remaining aware of your breathing, aware of each sip. In this way, your meditation will already have started.

Later in the day can be a nice time to sit for different reasons. While concentration may not be as good because of fatigue, it's a good time to release the concerns of the day and prepare for sleep. It's a time to let down, and let your body and mind recover from everything you were doing and thinking during the day.

How Long Should You Meditate?

To me, it's doubtful that you can learn to be happy in an open, mindful way without learning to meditate. Meditation is the basis. It provides the platform for learning to be mindful and happy in the rest of your life. How can you come back to mindfulness during your busy day if you haven't established it in some way to begin with? Without establishing a base for mindfulness through meditation, there's nothing to come back to.

Don't push yourself. To start, I'd rather have you meditate for five minutes with a sense of enjoyment about it than for two hours during which you are utterly miserable. I know too many people who have learned to meditate on strenuous retreats where you meditate for many hours each day. You might get a breakthrough. But if you're unprepared for the experience, you may not be able to integrate it, and six months later, you'll all too likely have stopped meditating. I've known many people who have had that experience.

If it doesn't feel too difficult, meditate for fifteen minutes or so to begin with, gradually lengthening the time as you get comfortable with the process. This allows sufficient time for your mental and physical formations to calm down significantly. And when you have learned to meditate for longer periods, *then* you may be ready for a meditation retreat. But, of course, if fifteen minutes is too difficult, start with five or ten. Start where you are. Make it pleasant so you will want to continue.

Meditation isn't a contest. It isn't really so much a matter of time. The most enlightened meditators aren't necessarily the ones who can sit the longest. Otherwise, chickens would be the most enlightened beings on the planet.

Sitting Meditation Practices

Here are some practices you can enjoy from the seated position.

─────── **Practice:** ───────
Enjoying the Breath

Sit in a comfortable position, as described previously. The point is to be upright but not rigid or tight, to be comfortable but alert.

Become aware of the state of your body and mind. What's going on with you right now? How have the things you have been doing and thinking affected your body and your consciousness? Just notice. If it feels okay to you, smile a gentle, Buddha-like smile, which helps your body and mind relax more deeply.

Then gently bring your attention down into your abdomen, just below the navel. Notice that your body is breathing in and out, in and out, all by itself. You don't have to make it go any special way. You can feel your diaphragm expanding and contracting, feel the air coming in and going out.

Now see if you can open to the *pleasantness* of these sensations. Breathing in is actually a delightful and refreshing feeling. It's like a cool drink on a hot day. Breathing out is a pleasant release, allowing tension and toxins to leave the body. Open to the happiness of just breathing.

Find what's interesting and pleasant about the breathing, and you will be able to enjoy it for a longer period of time and with greater concentration. Your attention *will* wander. That's just what minds do. There's nothing unusual or wrong about this, nothing to perturb yourself about. Simply notice the wandering with kind awareness, and when you can, gently bring your attention back to the breath without self-recrimination.

"Without self-recrimination" ultimately means that if feelings of self-judgment come up, you just notice them, practicing mere recognition. You know they are there, without fighting against them on the one hand, or indulging them on the other.

If you like, say "in" silently on each inbreath, and "out" on each outbreath to help focus your attention. When you don't need them, abandon the words like the raft by the stream. You can return to them later, when your attention wanders. It's often helpful to use words to direct your attention, but let them go when they start to feel burdensome. Let them lead you into silence. And when the silence becomes noisy, let them lead you back to silence.

Continue for an enjoyable period of time. Repeat this practice whenever you like.

—————— Practice: ——————
Breath Counting

Many Buddhists have found that counting the breath is helpful in developing concentration. The simplest way to do this is to just hold the number "one" in your mind throughout an inbreath and outbreath cycle. Then hold the number "two" in mind for the second cycle, and so on. If you lose count, go back to one. Go up to ten, and then begin again, if you'd like. If ten is too hard at first, try counting to five.

Remember that even as you count the breath, you can still enjoy the process. Sometimes I practice breath counting when I find myself especially distracted. After doing this a few times, I can enjoy my meditation more deeply.

—— Practice: ——
Using Words and Poetry

I used to have the prejudice that using words in meditation, which is sometimes called guided meditation, was an inferior method, a kind of crutch. But when I study some of the sutras, such as the Sutra on the Full Awareness of Breathing (*Ānāpānasati*), I find that the Buddha himself recommended this. Just as we use the insights of no self and impermanence not so much to substitute new concepts for old ones but to break up our usual habits of perception and come to a different place, so in meditation we can use words to come to silence. It's often wiser to give our busy minds something to do, some direction, rather than let them wander in the wilderness in a haze of confusion.

In many spiritual traditions, words can be a doorway into deep meditation. In Christianity, for example, there's a tradition known as *lectio divina*, literally, "divine reading." In this practice, you read a passage of scripture until something grabs your attention. It might be a phrase from a psalm, such as "The Lord is my light." If you feel this phrase pulling at your heart, pause and dwell with the entire phrase or just a portion, letting it water positive seeds in your consciousness: "The Lord is my light, my light, light," just letting the words wash over you, letting them fill you.

In Buddhist tradition, poetry is deeply connected to practice. Short poems called *gathas* are used to focus attention, perhaps through just breathing in and out while thinking of the phrases in the poem, or coordinating the breath with the lines of the poem so that you breathe in with one line and then breathe out with the next. This example is loosely based on the teachings of the Buddha in the Sutra on the Full Awareness of Breathing (Thich Nhat Hanh 1996). I have modified it here in accord with my own practice and insight.

> *Breathing in, breathing out.*
> *Aware of body.*
> *Calming body.*
> *Loving body.*
> *Letting everything go, letting everything be.*
> *Dwelling happily in the present moment.*
> *Dwelling serenely in the present moment.*
> *Everything is already here.*
> *Nothing is lacking.*
> *Everything is already here.*

You can write out these words to have them in front of you as you meditate. Let's take each verse step by step.

Breathing in, breathing out. To work with this poem, you begin by focusing on the breath. Let your inbreath refresh your body and mind. Let your outbreath release your tension and worry. Enjoy the sensations. Say "in" silently on each inbreath, and "out" on each outbreath. When your mind grows calm or when it begins to feel burdensome to stay with the words, just attend to each breath in silence. Stay with it for as long as you like, for your whole meditation period if it feels right. You aren't trying to get anywhere or accomplish anything. Each part of this gatha is as good as any other.

Aware of body. With your awareness still on the breath, let it broaden to include your whole body. Get a felt sense of your body as a whole, noticing exactly how things are with your body in this moment. If there's pain or tension in one area, note it. If your body feels pleasantly relaxed, just note it. Say the verse to yourself with every breath, then space it out to every second or third, and finally just attend silently to the body. When your awareness becomes scattered, return to the phrase.

Calming body. As your body begins to feel a little calmer, then you can switch to this verse. This phrase is not autosuggestion or self-hypnosis; it's a practice. That means you aren't trying to perform an end run around your conscious mind by cultivating calmness, but your conscious mind actively participates in inviting calmness into the body. It's simply a matter of watering the seeds of calmness that have already begun to arise. If you attend to the calm that is already present, it will tend to increase and deepen. Again, let the words fade into silence, returning to them when concentration fades.

Loving body. Bringing your attention to your body is already a kind of love. So this verse builds on what you are already doing. Invite a loving feeling to arise toward your body. If critical thoughts about your body arise, just notice and release them, and return to generating loving attention to your body, this amazing manifestation of the universe, this wonderful gift.

Letting everything go, letting everything be. As your worries arise, gently remind yourself to let go and let be. This is not struggling against having your worries or trying to make them go away. It's just letting them be the way they are without getting caught in them, seeing their nature as a changing pattern of energy in your consciousness. As you dwell with this verse, you might enjoy remembering the openness of the image of the Buddha seated with his bowl in front of him, an image of peace and acceptance.

Dwelling happily in the present moment. When your worries start to release their grip on you a little, releasing their pretense of being ultimate truth, you can invite your awareness to just open to the good things that are available within and around you in this moment. You can simplify the phrase as you proceed; for example, *Dwelling happily in the present moment, dwelling happily, happy....* Then let yourself return to silence if that feels comfortable for you.

Dwelling serenely in the present moment. Here you focus on the serenity that's already present, letting it increase in the same way. If you like, you can add other words of the same kind, such as "stillness," "harmony," "radiance," and so on; for example, *Dwelling in stillness, in harmony, in the radiance of the present...,* and so on.

Everything is already here. Since it's the nature of our intellect to carve reality into bits, for practical reasons spiritual teaching must divide indivisible reality into different aspects, distinguishing the ultimate (*dharmadhatu*) from the relative or historical (*lokadhatu*), the noumenal from the phenomenal. "Everything is already here" is a statement of ultimate truth rather than relative truth. In the relative dimension, we may feel that there's a lot lacking, that there are many things we need to have available that seem unavailable. But in the ultimate dimension, the dimension of the kingdom of heaven or the pure land of the Buddha, we know that everything is here and nothing is lacking. By touching one thing deeply, we touch everything. This verse can help lead you into contact with the ultimate dimension. But if you find yourself resisting it, or enumerating what's absent, don't fight it. Perhaps just return to the beginning of the poem. You can always work with this verse some other time.

Nothing is lacking. Everything is already here. These verses are a way of mentally rotating the insight of fullness and completeness in slightly different terms.

Meditation While Lying Down

Meditation while lying down can be especially relaxing.

─────── **Practice:** ───────
Body Scan Meditation

If you wish to try meditation in the lying-down position, this can be a very relaxing practice. Lie on a mat or other protective surface, something not so hard that it's uncomfortable. The mattress on your bed may be okay, or it might be a bit too soft for you to maintain clear awareness. Let your hands lie naturally by your sides, and let your feet fall away from each other. Don't use a pillow. The idea is to promote even and unimpeded blood flow throughout your body.

Bring your attention to your abdomen and feel your body breathe in and out exactly as it wants to, without your controlling it in any way. From the lying-down position, you can experience the rise and fall of the breath in a unique way, since as your abdomen expands, you can also feel your spine pressing against the mat or floor. After enjoying a few breaths, take your time while bringing your awareness down into your feet. Notice the sensations present in your feet, both on the surface and inside. Practice like this: "Breathing in, I'm aware of my feet. Breathing out, I smile to them." After the fist time, just shorten this to "feet, smiling." After a time, attend to your calves in the same way: "Breathing in, I'm aware of my calves. Breathing out I smile to my calves." "Calves, smiling." As you smile and breathe out, send loving-kindness to that part of your body, appreciating it, realizing all that it makes possible for you.

In the same way, practice with your thighs, hands, forearms, upper arms, neck and shoulders, facial muscles, eyes, ears, heart, lungs, stomach, and other digestive organs. You can use greater detail when you have more time and patience. For example, work with each foot or hand separately, or even each finger and toe, and each organ of the body, and so on.

When you're finished, breathe in and out, maintaining awareness of your body as a whole: "Breathing in, I'm aware of my whole body. Breathing out, I smile to my whole body."

Meditation While Walking

Walking meditation is a very enjoyable way to practice. I've found that it appeals to many in our culture, perhaps because we're more comfortable doing something than just sitting or lying down. Walking channels any nervous energy in the body, which makes it a good way for some people to begin learning meditation. It's also a nice transition from doing sitting meditation to engaging in daily activity.

Practice:
Walking Meditation

I like doing this practice informally. Walking meditation isn't about getting anywhere. It isn't about exercising. The purpose of walking meditation is to enjoy the walking. It's delightful to do this practice in a park or other natural setting, if possible. Walk in a relaxed way, taking your time. If you walk hurriedly, as you might for exercise, this gives your body and mind the message that you're tense and hurrying to get somewhere. So just walk slowly, at more of a stroll than a purposeful gait.

As you begin to walk, bring your attention down to the soles of your feet. Feel each contact your feet make with the earth as you walk. See about staying with that sensation, which will bring you away from the thinking mind. Simultaneously maintain awareness of your breathing. Measure your breath with your steps. How many steps do you naturally take on your inbreath? On your outbreath? It might, for example, be two steps for each. Or it might be two on the inbreath and three on the outbreath. This can also change as you go uphill or downhill. Always follow your body's needs rather than impose any particular count.

If you like, you can then also use a short gatha, coordinating it with your breathing and your steps. For example, say "in" silently on each inbreath and "out" on each outbreath. Or try "here" on the inbreath and "now" on the outbreath.

When you see something you like—the blue sky, a mountain, a beautiful flower, a tree—stop walking and just be present to that object for a while. Maintain awareness of your breath and your gatha as best you can, or you may get pulled out of the practice into your usual worries and preoccupations. (Of course, when this happens, just smile and remember to accept that experience too.)

Meditating While Standing

You can use similar approaches to meditate while standing.

———————— Practice: ————————
Awareness in the Standing Position

To practice while standing, just stand with your feet about shoulder-width apart. Notice the sensation of your contact with the ground or floor, and feel it hold you up. Enjoy your inbreath and outbreath a few times. Then expand your awareness to include both your breath and your whole body as you experience it in this position. You can scan the parts of your body as in the lying-down position, and then return to your sense of the body as a whole.

Sometimes you might like to tune in to your different senses as you stand, especially sound and sight. (You can also do this while sitting, lying down, or walking.) For a while, close your eyes and just focus on the sounds around you. See if you can become aware of the richness of even the most common, everyday sounds as you stand and breathe. I used to teach in a classroom in which the heating duct rattled, and people were aware of this as we worked with sound. Often people were surprised to learn that even such a sound, one that we normally might find a little grating or annoying, can be experienced as pleasant and interesting when you are simply open and aware, and don't resist what's happening.

After listening for a while, let your eyes open again. Notice the wonderful world of form and color, and just *receive* these sensations rather than try to reach out and grasp at them or cling to them.

The Five Hindrances

The Buddha talked about five major kinds of difficulties that can occur during meditation and other forms of training: sensory desire, hostility, dullness and lethargy, agitation and worry, and doubt. When your concentration isn't as good as you might prefer, check to see whether one or more of these hindrances is at work. Is the delicious smell of cooking food pulling you away from your meditation? Is anger interfering? Are you feeling dull or sleepy? Are you just anxious and worried? Or is doubt manifesting, perhaps in thoughts like "I don't get this," "This is a waste of time when I have so many things to do," or "I'm no good at this."

It's useful to recognize when one of the five hindrances is surfacing. Recognizing the problem as one of the five hindrances teaches that you aren't alone in having this difficulty. This is, in fact, familiar territory, territory everyone who has learned to meditate through the centuries has also encountered. When one of these hindrances comes up, the practice is, as always, mere recognition and acceptance: "Right now, there's worry coming up," "Right now, there's a pull from sensations that are occupying my awareness," and so on. Using the words "right now" gently reminds you that these phenomena are impermanent, like everything else, and don't need to be fought against.

Transitioning

Avoid treating meditation as just another item on your to-do list that you can check off once you've finished so you can move on to your normal, nonmindful way of doing things. The transition moments from daily life to meditation and from meditation to daily life are important liminal moments. When settling into meditation, allow yourself some time. Take an unhurried look around you. When your eyes close, keep in touch with your surroundings by noting the sounds you hear. Don't "hurry up and meditate." When you complete your meditation period, form a clear intention to bring the meditation with you into whatever comes next as best you can, bringing a contemplative attitude into daily life.

Please Remember

In this chapter, you have been introduced to a number of different kinds of meditation practices. Take your time in experimenting with these different approaches. Have fun with it. Remember to practice with acceptance, peace, and happiness. Don't struggle against your wandering mind or whatever's coming up in your awareness, but gently, kindly, and persistently keep bringing the mind back to the focus of your meditation. Let go of any idea of meditating perfectly. The idea of perfection introduces a goal orientation that's incompatible with this activity, whose essence is *just being*. Concentration will improve naturally if you are patient, accepting yourself as you are and accepting whatever arises. Give it time. Meditation goes against the grain of a lifetime of doing, accomplishing, and sensory overload. It takes a little while to train yourself to do something new.

chapter 8

Living Happiness

Every step of the way to heaven is heaven.

—St. Catharine of Siena

Many people remember the scam Tom Sawyer pulled on his friends in Mark Twain's novel *The Adventures of Tom Sawyer.* To avoid the work of whitewashing the fence, Tom managed to convince his friends that he loved doing this chore and wouldn't give it up for the world. He even acted reluctant to let them pitch in, as if not doing the task himself amounted to a huge sacrifice.

Tom Sawyer scammed himself more than he did his friends. Whitewashing the fence can be enjoyable. It depends entirely on your attitude. If you approach such an activity solely as a means activity—merely as something you have to do to accomplish a goal—you miss all the moments of whitewashing the fence. But if you approach it as an ends activity—something that's done for its own sake, not just as a means to an end—all those moments of working on the fence remain yours to enjoy. They become worthwhile moments of life, moments when you are alive in the present moment.

To reclaim all the moments of our lives requires the capacity to *enjoy* doing whatever we do, to find the intrinsic pleasantness contained therein. Instead of treating our moments as simply empty time to suffer through on the way to our goals, we can learn to focus on the pleasurable aspects of each activity. We can learn to say to ourselves, "enjoying doing the laundry," instead of, "I have to wash theses clothes before I can watch TV." We can learn to say, "enjoying reading my e-mail," "enjoying returning my phone calls," or "enjoying driving to work," not using these words to deny our present experience but to open the door to a different kind of experience, an experience where we attend to what's pleasant in the present moment. Just as we can learn to enjoy our meditation, we can also bring that same spirit into daily life and be deeply in touch with what's happening right now in our bodies and minds and all around us.

Just as we can hear birdsong as either neutral, background sound or something pleasant, wonderful, or even amazing, depending on the quality of our attention, we can convert every task we face in daily life from neutral or even unpleasant to something we can enjoy.

The Paradox of Practice

Viewed from one angle, living mindfully and happily is the easiest thing in the world. Viewed from another angle, it's quite challenging. Remembering both aspects of this paradox helps us to approach practice in a sane way, without becoming frustrated or giving up.

Practice Is Easy

We have to remember the easiness of practice. Fundamentally, it's about relaxing into the present moment. It's about being present, and instead of searching endlessly for what we feel is lacking or running away from what we dislike, simply opening to the happiness that is already there, available, waiting for us.

In this moment, I hear the sound of water running off the roof from the snow that just fell. I can hear the sounds of the workmen downstairs. I hear the washer and dryer. I hear the clickety-clack of my computer keys as I write. The coffee in my cup is now cold, but still tastes good. I'm in good health. My body is seated comfortably. I'm comfortably warm on this cold January day. All in all, it's a wonderful moment.

I could easily have a different experience in this same situation. If I resisted my experience, I could wonder, "When in the world are they ever going to finish up that work?" I could resist the sounds of the washer and dryer or the water running off the roof. I could remain unaware that my body is warm and comfortable. I could get caught up in complaining that my coffee is cold or in wishing that my computer keys didn't make so much noise. It all depends on the quality of consciousness I bring to this situation.

In this sense, living mindfully and happily is simple. I only need to remember to be mindful and open. The practice is ease itself. When I remember this, I know I can learn to be mindful and open in every moment. Every moment can become a valued experience of being alive.

Being mindful and open is also so much easier—that is, so much more full of ease—than moments when we get caught up in struggling and resisting. By just remaining open, by remembering to enjoy what's present, we can do everything in a way that's healing and nurturing. We remember ourselves. We are present and aware. Zen master Lin-chi (died 867) put it like this:

There is no place in Buddhism for using effort. Just be ordinary, and nothing special. Relieve your bowels, pass water, put on your clothes, eat your food. When you're tired, go and lie down. Ignorant people may laugh at me, but the wise will understand.... As you go from place to place, if you regard each one as your own home, they will all be genuine, for when circumstances come, you must not try to change them. Then your usual habits of feeling, which make karma for the five hells, will of themselves become the great ocean of liberation (Watts 1957, 101).

In this sense, practice is easy. It's about knowing your own nature and following it, not working against yourself. In a sense, it's the easiest thing of all. Remembering this can give you a lot of encouragement.

Practice Is Difficult

There's another side, however. From this angle, nothing is more difficult than Lin-chi's injunction to be natural. The moment we attempt to be natural, we no longer even know what natural is.

Anyone who takes seriously the teaching to be mindful and aware moment by moment quickly comes to see that this is challenging. So many alluring things are around to distract us, so many difficult things to frustrate and worry us, so many things to pull us away from mindfulness. We try to be mindful, only to suddenly get pulled away again. In the beginning, hours can go by before we remember our intention to be aware. We return briefly, and then very quickly fall into distraction again, sometimes within the space of one breath.

What makes the practice seem difficult is our drivenness and perfectionism. If you keep falling away from mindfulness and coming back to it, this isn't a problem. What makes it a problem is when we approach the practice the same way we approach the rest of life. We want to *achieve* mindfulness. We want to become *really good* at it. In this way, ego slips in, and we treat being happy in the present moment as one more goal to strive for.

Just Take One Step

We avoid the trap of seeing practice as difficult, and recover a sense of naturalness and ease in it when we take a *process orientation*. In a process orientation, we're not trying to achieve anything special. We remind ourselves that the Buddha's practice is non-practice and that he gained nothing from total enlightenment. All that matters is being mindful *now*, in this very moment. In this sense, it doesn't matter if you weren't mindful for the past three hours, and it doesn't matter if you fall into forgetfulness again for the next three. All you can do, all you have to do, is be mindful right now.

When you walk, see about taking just one mindful step, one step where you are completely present to the walking, where you feel your body's movements, feel each of your feet caress the earth when it touches down. Just take one mindful breath, remaining completely present to these pleasant sensations. When you prepare a meal, just do each step with full awareness. And that's enough. Don't get caught up in evaluating. Just do the next thing at hand with mindfulness.

We cause ourselves distress when we forget either side of this paradox. When the practice seems difficult, we become frustrated. If we imagine it should be so easy that we could just hear about the practice and immediately do it continuously, we might despair. Be kind and patient with yourself. Just come back to this thing, right now, right here.

Start of Day

Just as a toddler uses her mother as home base, coming back to her before going off on more playful adventures, so we adults need a home base as well. Our home base is mindfulness. We need a way to start off the day by establishing mindfulness as soon as we wake up. We need to spend some time making contact with mindfulness before getting caught up in the busyness of the day. We can't return to a home base we haven't established.

I like to recite a gatha the moment I get out of bed, which strengthens my intention to live the day mindfully. Following is a morning gatha I wrote for you. You can write it down and place it where you can see it easily when you get up in the morning. It's short enough that if you use it every day, you will have it memorized before long. Breathe in and out with the text, letting the meaning touch you. Pause between the lines. If you find yourself repeating the words mechanically, go over the gatha again in a way that helps you set your deep intention for the day.

> *This is a new day.*
> *Let me live this day mindfully and deeply.*
> *Let me take my time and not rush.*
> *Let me see each being with kindness.*

As part of your home base, see about finding some time in the morning to meditate. I know mornings can be a rushed time in many households, as we prepare for work. But even if you can only meditate for a few moments, that's much better than nothing. Having some base to return to is much better than having none.

Reading

Reading things that inspire you to be mindful, happy, and aware is a very important practice. When you find a book that inspires you, treat it as a treasure. Keep it in a special place. Don't be content with just one reading, but come back to it again and again. Good books contain layers of meaning and insight, and each reading can reveal something new to you. As you find additional helpful books, keep them in the same place. Rotate through these books. Since you have selected books that speak to you, often just reading a page or two can help immensely to establish your base in the morning, and again later in the day, if you wish. Inspiring books also help you prepare for meditation.

Your Personal Bible

In your reading, from time to time you might find a passage that speaks to you. Mark it. Slowly read it over to yourself, breathing in and out, and letting the meaning penetrate you. Then write out the passage in a special notebook, contemplating it again as you write. Once your book begins to fill up, it becomes a powerful tool for transformation. Since you've selected every passage, you can open your book to any page and find something that will encourage and inspire you, something that will help you stay with your intention to live deeply.

Please don't underestimate the value of this practice. Simple as it may seem, it's one of the most important things you can do in your process of transformation.

Stopping

Given that practice is a matter of returning again and again to mindfulness from moments of forgetfulness, it helps to pause frequently during the day. Now and then, stop in the middle of a task and take a few mindful breaths right where you are. If you're walking from the kitchen to the living room, stop halfway and take three or four mindful breaths. See if you can maintain mindfulness as you start walking again, taking care to be fully mindful for at least three breaths from the time when you paused. Likewise, in the middle of showering, stop and breathe. Feel the warm water running over you. You can build this kind of pause into many activities, noting the quality of the habit energy that presses you to complete the task at hand while also establishing your freedom and learning that you don't have to be pushed by habit energy.

In addition to stopping briefly in the middle of tasks, look for natural pauses that occur during the day. Do you have to stop for a red traffic light? Now, rather than being an inconvenience, the traffic light becomes the Buddha calling you back to mindfulness. Are you waiting for your computer to boot up? Are you waiting in a line at the grocery or bank? These are opportunities to breathe, smile, and return to yourself. If your situation allows, it's wonderful to pause and breathe about every fifteen minutes. It doesn't take a lot of time.

Coming to Your Senses

When we get caught in our constant mental chatter, we lose ourselves. To return to ourselves means to come back to direct sensory experience instead of getting lost in our thinking. One way to do this is to concentrate on several areas of your body. Sitting upright in a chair, stop and breathe. Focus on the sensation of your hair (or skin) on your head. Feel exactly what that sensation is like. After a few moments, focus on the feeling of your clothing against your shoulders. Pause and breathe as you focus on these sensations for a while. Then focus on the chair against your back. In the same way, focus on the feeling of your clothing against the tops of your thighs. Then focus on the feeling of your shoes on your feet. Repeat this if you have time, tuning in to the sensation of your hair, shoulders, back, thighs, and feet. Now focus on your body as a whole. Notice the effect of completing this simple exercise. It's surprisingly powerful.

Continuous Full Attention

Ours is an age of distraction and multitasking. We have become a society of continuous partial attention. We never just do what we're doing, but we're always doing something else as well. We watch television, talk on the phone, text, and eat a snack all at the same time.

Instead, mindfulness invites single tasking. You have the right to just eat lunch and enjoy eating lunch. You don't have to answer e-mails and talk on the phone at the same time. If you're watching a film you enjoy, you have the right to be present and soak in it. You have the right to walk in the direction of continuous full attention. In this way, you can avoid the treadmill of the endless busyness of life. It may take a little while to patiently reeducate your nervous system, which has become used to extreme and continuous levels of stimulation, but it's worth it.

Awareness of Others

Many times we become so busy or so focused on other things that we scarcely acknowledge the presence of other people *as people*. We may scarcely see the clerk at the bank, the person who waits on us at lunch, or the driver in the next car at a traffic light. A wonderful practice is to notice that there's another human being there whenever you have contact with someone, however briefly. Pause and make eye contact with that person if possible. Say inwardly, "I see you." You may be surprised how this pulls you out of your distraction. What's more, people respond to this practice right away. They seem to like being seen.

Mindfulness of Kindness

Every day, we are the recipients of countless acts of kindness. Someone smiles at us. Someone holds a door open for us. Someone lets us into a line of traffic. There's kindness in the simple presence of a partner or friend. It's an act of kindness even when others are simply doing their jobs, for example, the person who picks up the trash, the one who delivers our mail or packages, someone on the phone who is courteous and helpful. Given the brain's negative bias, it's very easy for us to focus on the difficulties other people cause us. It's very important to focus on the opposite when it occurs. And, once you start to notice, you'll see that it occurs a lot.

Protecting Your Body and Mind

Every day, we expose ourselves to countless toxins, not only in what we eat and drink but also through the media we encounter. Without aiming for any rigid perfection about it, see if you can go in the direction of consuming only what's helpful to your body and mind. Limit your exposure to dark, despairing, or violent television, films, and reading material, anything that waters the seeds of sorrow in you. Sometimes you may find it helpful to limit your exposure to the news, which is often driven by fear and sensationalism. And when you do watch the news, protect yourself with the shield of compassion and equanimity. Know that the stories of suffering you see are your story, *our* story, not something remote or abstract. Books and films containing cynicism and despair get better reviews in our culture, but still contaminate the heart and diminish our well-being, whatever their supposed artistic merit.

Exercise is another important form of protection for our bodies and minds. It not only rids the body of waste products and protects our health, but also helps us to be mindful. Whether we like hiking or jogging, yoga or tai chi, after a good workout, we feel calm, cleansed, and at ease. In this state, being mindful is much easier.

Finding Refuge

We are buffeted in life by what Buddhists call the eight winds: gain and loss, praise and dishonor, flattery and disgrace, pain and joy. Of course, loss, dishonor, disgrace, and pain are troubling. But even the positive wind in each pair can cause suffering if it triggers clinging. The teaching of the eight winds reveals that these things are predictable and natural, not just for some of us but for all of us. To find peace, we need to let them blow without being blown away by them.

To prevent becoming overwhelmed by these winds, Buddhists take refuge in the three jewels: the Buddha, the dharma, and the sangha. They take refuge in the one who shows the way of understanding and love, in the teaching, and in the community that puts that teaching into practice. You, too, can take refuge in the three jewels. But you can also take refuge in your own heritage. Take refuge in God, who protects and loves you, or Christ, the divine light, or whatever helps you feel safe. When you feel unsafe, it's difficult to be mindful.

The Six Pāramitās

The Buddha offered the teaching of the six *pāramitās*, or six perfections, as a helpful guide for daily life: *dāna* pāramitā, *shīla* pāramitā, *kshanti* pāramitā, *vīrya* pāramitā, *dhyāna* pāramitā, and *prajñā* pāramitā. You can use this wonderful teaching as a guide for your daily life.

Dāna Pāramitā

Dāna means "generosity." When we live in a generous way, we break down the sense of separateness, the illusion of being an isolated and alienated self, cut off from the rest of the universe. On the other hand, living in a selfish way strengthens the illusion of separation. Every time we act out of selfishness, it convinces us more deeply that we live in a world of aggression, hostility, and alienation.

We can practice generosity each day. It's not just about giving extraordinary gifts. A smile is an act of generosity. Just being a little tolerant with someone who is upset and not in best form is a generous deed. Letting someone in the door ahead of you even though you'll be farther behind in the line is a generous act. There are innumerable ways to practice dāna.

Generosity is a powerful remedy. You will benefit from it even more than those with whom you're generous.

Shīla Pāramitā

Shila means precepts. The traditional basic precepts in Buddhism involve not killing, not stealing, avoiding illicit sexual behavior, being truthful, and refraining from intoxicants. Rather than merely rules imposed from the outside, these are viewed as practices you appropriate through your own insight.

Whether or not you want to follow these traditional precepts, consider what your own precepts would be, based on insight into your own life and situation. Some precepts you might consider in seeking to live mindfully are allowing time so you don't have to rush, slowing down, accepting whatever tasks are at hand without reluctance, bringing deep awareness to everything you do, single tasking, practicing awareness of your breath while performing daily tasks, being mindful of kindness, and pausing frequently to enjoy your breathing.

Precepts protect us when our wisdom is otherwise too shallow or inconsistent to do so. They keep us from the cliff's edge, from falling into many difficulties.

Kshanti Pāramitā

Kshanti may be translated as "inclusiveness." Our consciousness is forever drawing lines in the sand, saying this is acceptable, but that is beyond the pale, something we can't accept. Often we treat other people as being outside the line of what we find acceptable, perhaps because they're of another religion or political philosophy. We even treat some of our own thoughts and mental states as unacceptable, for example, when we try to repress worries or sad thoughts rather than embrace them mindfully.

Kshanti pāramitā challenges us to leave nothing outside the line of our compassion and understanding.

Vīrya Pāramitā

Vīrya means "diligence," "energy," or "perseverance." We practice vīrya by kindly attending to our consciousness, encouraging positive seeds and avoiding toxic input that promotes unwholesome mental states. The diligence here should be gentle and steady rather than forced or violent.

Dhyāna Pāramitā

Dhyāna refers to "mental training" or "meditation." It's very beneficial to include some time each day for meditation, establishing the base for mindfulness during the rest of our activities.

Prajñā Pāramitā

Prajñā means "wisdom." This can mean approaching daily life in a wise, nonreactive way, without allowing the eight winds to blow us apart, without letting our thoughts and emotions pull us into destructive speech and action. In particular, prajñā refers to the wisdom of impermanence and no self, learning to view everything we experience in the light of these seminal insights. See everything in life as a kind of passing dream or phantom. For in the light of impermanence and no self, that is closer to the truth.

End of Day

After your busy day of going, doing, and working, it's helpful to give yourself some peaceful time in the evening. Let your body and mind rest and restore themselves. They know how to do that if given a chance. Don't let yourself be invaded by toxic media all evening long.

Evening is a wonderful time to do body scan meditation, letting the tensions of the day fall away. Perhaps you would like to listen to healing music or do a walking meditation. You don't have to make rigid rules, but if you watch television or read, or whatever else you do, be aware of its effect on you. Let your mindfulness guide you into doing more of what's healing and nourishing, and less of what fills you with tension.

When we go to sleep at night, sometimes our worries about the day just behind us or ahead of us come up powerfully in our awareness. Just notice them without resisting: "There's a worry coming up about…," "I'm aware of planning what I need to do tomorrow," and so on. In addition to caring for your worries through mere recognition, also remind yourself of what was good during the day. Note any steps you were able to take toward living more mindfully.

If you wake up in the night, don't just lie there tossing and turning. Get up and practice sitting meditation for fifteen to twenty minutes. Lying there half asleep, you're likely to find repetitive thoughts and worries looping interminably in your consciousness. The sitting posture helps you reclaim enough consciousness and clarity to bring mindfulness to whatever's going on and allow it to calm down by embracing it. It will help even if your fatigue makes you feel that you're not meditating well (how pervasive our self-judgments are!).

One Thing

In the New Testament, we read the account of two sisters who receive Jesus into their home. Martha is busy serving their guest, while Mary sits and listens attentively to his teaching. Martha complains to Jesus, asking him to tell her sister to help with her many responsibilities. Instead, he replies that Mary has made the better choice. "Martha, Martha, you are anxious and troubled by many things; *one thing is needful*. Mary has chosen the good portion, which shall not be taken away from her" (Luke 10:38–42, Revised Standard Version; italics added). In other words, instead of all our busyness, the simplicity of attending to what is most important— here the presence and teaching of Christ—is what really matters. Even doing good deeds can detract from our higher purpose.

In the teachings of Buddhism, there are many practices and insights that are difficult to understand and to penetrate when you first encounter them. Don't let this worry you. Only one thing is really needed: to live our daily lives deeply and mindfully. When we dedicate ourselves to this one task, the rest of life becomes clear. We begin to know what to do and what to avoid doing. We don't miss our lives from being lost in the past or future, lost in our regrets or worries. When we live mindfully, we become aware of our impermanent and selfless nature, and that of everything around us.

With the many things we have to do and remember each day, it's freeing to remember that our overarching goal is this one simple thing. Ultimately the only thing we need to remember is to be mindful, which means to be fully alive, to remember ourselves and our lives, to avoid losing ourselves in distraction and scattered thoughts and being pulled in so many different directions. We love God by being fully alive. We gain eternal life, not conceived as an endless extension of time but as a quality of life that is full and deep.

chapter 9

Death and Rebirth

*Free thyself from the past, free thyself from the future, free thyself
from the present. Crossing to the farther shore of existence, with
mind released everywhere, no more shalt thou come to birth and
decay.*

—Buddha

There's a monster lurking in the shadows and back alleys of your
mind. You seldom catch a glimpse of it, but its presence influences
what you do and how you feel in every aspect of your life. To avoid
it, you busy yourself with planning, grasping, clinging, and avoiding, always trying to anticipate where the monster might show up
so you can stay out of its reach. Because of this creeping darkness,
you can never quite be happy or fully at ease.

The monster is death, not in some vague, abstract sense, but death itself, death in the singular—your death, my death. Until we can confront this beast, we're doomed to a state of anxiety and fear.

The Wisdom of Knowing

By considering the accounts of the deaths of great spiritual teachers, reincarnation, and past-life regression, we can get a sense of what can be known about death.

How a Master Dies

Yongey Mingyur Rinpoche (2007) recounts the story of the 1981 death of a realized Tibetan Buddhist teacher known as the Sixteenth Karmapa. Despite suffering from a horrible form of cancer, he never complained of pain, but seemed far more interested in the well-being of the hospital staff who came by frequently, outside the scope of their medical duties, to experience the enormous peace he radiated.

When he died, his companions requested that his body be left undisturbed for three days—a difficult request for a modern hospital to accommodate. They left him seated on his bed in the meditation posture in which he had died. His body never entered rigor mortis, and the area around his heart stayed preternaturally warm, almost as warm as in life. Even twenty years later, his body remained inexplicably intact, defying scientific explanation.

Sushila Blackman (2005) compiled many accounts similar to that of the Sixteenth Karmapa. But perhaps the strangest thing isn't Blackman's work so much as Blackman herself. While working on the book, she was diagnosed with advanced lung cancer, and died just a month and a half after finishing. Somehow, it seems she intuited that she needed to write this book in preparation for her own death.

Accounts of Reincarnation

In April 1950, a ten-year-old boy from the Jain family, named Nirmal, died of smallpox in the village of Kosi Kalan in Uttar Pradesh, India (Stevenson 1974). In his delirium, he told his mother, "You are not my mother," and said he was going to his real mother. Though he didn't actually name it, as he said this, he pointed in the direction of a small town called Chhatta, about six miles away. A short time later, he died.

A year and a few months later, a boy was born to the Varshnay family in Chhatta. They named him Prakash. At four and a half, he began waking up in the middle of the night, running out of the house, and saying he belonged to Kosi Kalan and his name was Nirmal. He correctly named Nirmal's father, sister, and other family members and friends.

While not everyone will be convinced this was reincarnation, the facts aren't easily explained, and there are many other such accounts. Some, like the case of Prakash, or Nirmal, were studied in a rigorous and systematic way.

Past-Life Regression

Brian Weiss (1988), a scientifically trained psychiatrist, encountered a case where a woman he called Catherine regressed under hypnosis and reported memories of a past life. These memories brought healing of present-day symptoms. In spite of his initial skepticism, Weiss then began to discover many other such cases.

The Wisdom of Not Knowing

Once a young Zen student asked his elderly teacher what happened after death. "I don't know," said the old man.

"But you're a Zen master!" exclaimed the surprised student.

"Yes," said the teacher, "I'm a Zen master—but not a dead one."

With the simplicity and directness characteristic of Buddhism in general, and Zen in particular, the master speaks the truth. Who knows what happens after death? And yet the student's question is an important one, for if we knew the answer, maybe we wouldn't be so afraid—not only of death but also of life.

In Buddhism the greatest gift is the gift of no fear. How can we be anything but afraid without knowing what death holds for us? We can pretend to be unafraid or try to avoid thinking about it. But fear of death and the resulting denial we try to use against it distorts our awareness, creating a background of barely acknowledged but pervasive tension and anxiety (Becker 1973).

As human beings, we occupy a unique niche. We are life aware of itself. We are life aware of its limits. Able to contemplate infinity, able to touch eternity, we yet know ourselves as finite and temporary. As far as we can tell, we're the only animals on the planet with that kind of awareness. Those willing to consider the question posed by our finitude and impermanence are spiritual people at heart; those unwilling to do this, however often they go to church or do outwardly religious things, are not.

When we don't acknowledge the truth of our human situation, we pretend we will live this same life forever. When we deny death, it seems to make sense to accumulate things: wealth, prestige, pleasure, and power. We seem to feel that these things will always be ours to keep. Though we say, "You can't take it with you," we act as though we could.

When we take seriously that life ends, we question the wisdom of making such things the central facts of our existence. Such things are in no way evil or wrong—just distractions that, if we aren't careful about them, can lead us away from living deeply.

The accumulation of things relates to a larger strategy we use to avoid looking at our human situation and its limits. It's part of the ploy of *specialness*. All of us are infected with this conceit to some extent. When we look into our own thoughts, we can often find ourselves thinking and acting as if, while everyone else might grow old, get sick, and die sooner or later, we ourselves are somehow immune. We stand outside such ills, remarkably somehow not reflecting on the fact that, if we actually *were* immune, we'd be the first. It's extremely difficult to grasp, while alive and vital, that we will die, that this is not a fable or a vague idea, but a concrete, inescapable, and unavoidable fact. Though we say nothing is certain but death and taxes, even this makes light of the matter, as if death were merely an annoyance like taxation, rather than the ultimate question.

If specialness is the first distortion we use to try to avoid awareness of death, there's a second kind of distortion closely related to it. If we don't feel secure in our specialness, we use the distortion of *dependence* on someone or others we imagine to be special. Ultimately, our fascination with celebrities is symptomatic of just this sort of trick. We become fascinated with their lives, as if they were Olympian gods and goddesses, as if we hope that by following their fortunes and misfortunes, their DWIs and affairs, we too will become immortals.

Death as Liberator

Caution is in order so that our beliefs don't obscure the reality of death. We must come to terms with the finality of death—not just death in general or at some far-off time, but our own very particular, very concrete, and not necessarily so distant demise. Otherwise, death can't serve its function as liberator. If you take your hand and feel the bony lower-back part of your skull, or touch the bones in your other hand, you can see that, like other mortal beings, you are bone. In this way, you open the door to knowing directly that one day, bone is all that will be left of you and at some later point, not even that.

This is where we start. Otherwise our beliefs about continuation after death are only a form of denial, permitting us to continue struggling, striving, and acquiring. For this reason, Buddhist monks and nuns remind themselves daily that they will grow old, get sick, and die; that in the end, since everything is impermanent, they will lose all they love and hold dear; and that the only thing we truly own is our deeds (*karma*). For these are what shape the flow and pattern of our energy streaming into the future. Don't misunderstand: This is no dispiriting, negative practice. It's a liberating one, one that frees us to be alive and avoid illusion.

By knowing clearly that we must die, we can be fully alive. Knowing death gives us the wisdom to want to avoid wasting our days. It teaches us to be awake every moment, to appreciate life without just running through it to get to some imagined future. Death teaches us to be alive now, and now is the only time we can be alive. We shouldn't squander life by always struggling for some never-arriving tomorrow.

So from this perspective, we can consider the wisdom and honesty of our aged Zen master who said he didn't know what happens after death. What happens when we die? Who knows? Thus he reminds us not to get caught up in speculation, but to live. If we can acknowledge death with serenity, what's left to fear? You don't have to struggle to be special. You don't have to cling to those you imagine are special. You know your own life is a miracle. You learn to breathe and smile, to see the good available in every moment and circumstance, and to become truly happy in your actual life, maybe for the first time.

At the level of relative truth, death is the hard fact of our existence and our unavoidable fate. Though at the ultimate level of truth, we might have inklings of immortality through the accounts of the deaths of great spiritual teachers, reincarnation, and past-life regression, or through our own experience and insight, these should not be used to distort the fact that death involves a real ending at another level. When we forget death, we forget to be alive, here and now.

How many times has someone tried to console a grieving person by saying the deceased has "gone on to a better place" or something similar? Sometimes the griever can take in the kind intent behind such remarks and even feel encouraged by them. But many times, such stock phrases subtly, or not so subtly, cause grievers to feel even more alone, creating the feeling that no one really understands the concreteness of their loss, the depth of their sorrow. At the ultimate level of truth, death is not just an ending. But this insight must never be used to contribute to our denial and distortion. When someone dies, something has really happened. Something has been lost.

At the same time, death is not as unfamiliar to us as we might sometimes imagine. In the process of deep psychotherapy, death often shows up in the room. Paul is an example.

Death in Psychotherapy: The Story of Paul

Paul came to therapy after an incident in which he became enraged on the road. At first he was not at all convinced that his anger was really a problem. To him, it seemed fully justified and reasonable. But somehow, for reasons he could only dimly grasp, it seemed to be a problem for the people around him. Paul left in his wake a string of broken relationships, disappointed friendships, and sudden job terminations. Once he turned thirty-five, he started to notice the pattern.

Over many months, Paul went back and forth, at times starting to glimpse that his anger was problematic and painful, other times unable to see why people reacted negatively to it. His anger made him feel powerful and in control, as if he were protecting the tender, sensitive feelings of vulnerability and fears of mortality underneath. He prided himself on his anger, and was glad he wasn't some lowly sheep who mindlessly accepted injustice. At one point, he told me that giving up his angry self felt like dying. It scared him. It seemed as if he were giving up the best of himself, the very thing that made him special. Eventually he sensed that the death of his angry self, so focused on feeling powerful in the face of real and imagined injustice, was not only an ending but also a beginning. He realized that dying to this self also meant being born as a calmer, kinder person, someone who could still stand up for himself and others but who didn't need to approach every situation in a full suit of armor with sword drawn.

The sense that change is like dying comes in many forms. People may discover that their narrow childhood religions no longer work for them and must be left behind. They also experience this as a kind of death, relinquishing something that once comforted them. Sometimes people who consider themselves materialists spontaneously discover the spiritual side of their lives, and are frightened by it. People may find that they are more than the traditional gender roles they had previously accepted. In all these discoveries, there's an element of grief: the old way of being is no longer adequate, and must die. There's a feeling of self-betrayal in having limited ourselves by clinging to old frameworks. The seventy-five-year-old wishes he could have discovered these things at forty, and the forty-year-old regrets she didn't discover them when she was twenty. But whether it happens early or late, the process is a kind of dying. The accommodations of the past no longer suffice. There's a need to stop clinging to old ways and embrace a wider vision.

Death and Resurrection

Mindfulness is a way of life, a way of being happy and fully alive. It's also a path of transformation. And transformation entails an element of dying. While I am being mindful, enjoying the warm sunlight, the sparkling water, or majestic mountains, in that same moment I have died to my usual worries and preoccupations. One can feel a strange sense of loss about this, as if to say, "If I'm no longer the person who was so full of fear and worry, anger, self-doubt, or whatever other limiting view I had of myself, then who am I?" In the moment of such a realization, the earth moves beneath us. The foundations shake. We are crucified, transformed, resurrected. We die. And we are reborn.

Whether we encounter it in Christian tradition, in the Egyptian story of the death and resurrection of Osiris, or somewhere else, something in us responds to the theme of death and resurrection. We respond to it because it's nothing arbitrary. It's an archetype, knit into the very fabric of the psyche. The cells in our bodies are continually dying while new cells are being born. Our consciousness changes from moment to moment. We die every second, and we are reborn every second.

From this perspective, we catch a glimpse of the realization that death is really a name for transformation. It's not as unfamiliar as we imagine; it's something we experience continually. Seeing this, we are ready to understand what death is, without falling either into denial and distortion, on the one hand, or despair and cynicism on the other.

Rebirth

The Heart Sutra says nothing is produced and nothing is destroyed. Reality is actually a selfless, undividable, continually impermanent and transforming "that." "That" is ultimately unnamable and unknowable. Buddhists don't even try. When we try to name it, we create many problems. Once we name it, we fall into the delusion of thinking we know what we're talking about. We may even think that in some sense, it's ours, that we have it and own it, and that other people, who use different words and concepts, are all wrong about it.

Jewish piety hints at this insight from a different angle. Jews have a name for "that," the well-known tetragrammaton consisting of the four Hebrew letters that constitute God's proper name. This name is considered so holy that many pious Jews won't pronounce it. ("Jehovah," though, is undoubtedly incorrect.) Instead of saying it aloud, Jews say *Adonai* (the Lord) or even just *Hashem* (the Name). Often the letters of God's name aren't even fully written out, even in English, a reminder that ultimately we don't really know what we're talking about when we talk about "that," and in the end, we might be better off just keeping quiet, being mindful, breathing, and smiling.

Buddhists call what happens after death "rebirth" rather than "reincarnation." Reincarnation literally means "back into the flesh," and in light of the insight of no self, what is it, after all, that goes and comes back? If you are not a separate self but are an indivisible manifestation of "that," where could you ever go, and how could you ever return? And what is this "you" anyway? "Rebirth" is perhaps a little better, but still conveys a problematic sense of our being some sort of separate something that leaves and returns.

Rebirth and No Self

You are not a separate, alienated, lost, and alone bit of a someone or something adrift in the universe. You're not separate at all. You're formed entirely from stuff you usually think isn't you. You, as a living being, are formed entirely from what you normally think of as nonliving water and a few pounds of nonliving minerals. What you really are is a patterned flow of energy, a process of transformation and change that's never the same from one moment to the next. What you think of as you is actually composed of everything else in the universe. And if that's what you really are, what is it that's reincarnated or reborn?

When you consider rebirth in this light, you are several million light-years away from thinking that in the past you were, in any simplistic sense, Cleopatra or Julius Caesar, Bach or Beethoven. It's not so clear what such statements might refer to. Does some subtle energy pattern jump across from one life to another, even allowing, in some cases, memory of the prior life? Perhaps so. But can we call this energy pattern "you" in the way you normally think of yourself?

One of the fabulous games the human mind can play is to engage in questions contrary to fact, in what-ifs. "What if," we might say, "I'd been born to wealthy parents and gone to Yale? How would my life be different? What opportunities might I have had if I'd hobnobbed with George Bush and John Kerry in the Skull and Bones? What doors would have opened to me?" Or we can ask, "What if I'd been born with great athletic ability?" "What if I'd had perfect, nurturing parents?" or "What if I'd been best friends with John, Paul, George, and Ringo back in Liverpool, and they'd asked me to join the group?"

These may be intriguing questions, but just because our wonderful brains can perform such mental gymnastics doesn't show that they mean anything. If you'd gone to Yale, you would have been someone else, not you. Part of what makes you who you are is that you had the experiences you had and not some other experiences. What if you'd had a more athletic body? Then, once again, you would not be you, would you? You'd be someone else. Body and consciousness are a unity. If you'd had a different body, you'd have a different consciousness too. Having that body would have changed your experiences and your consciousness. You would not be you. Nor would you be you if you were the fifth Beatle, because that, too, would have changed you.

So in this light, what does it mean if we say you were once someone else, living in a different time or place, and now you have come back and are living *this* life, in *this* time and circumstance, in *this* body? The truth is, being in a certain body in a particular time and place with a specific set of genes and experiences is all part of what makes you *you*; is it not?

Perhaps by now (if I've done my job), your head is spinning a bit. But maybe in that spinning, you're gaining respect for the old Zen teacher who said he didn't know what happens after death. Maybe you're loosening your grip on your concepts a little. The Buddha always encourages us to let go of our concepts in favor of direct perception of reality—only so can we find happiness.

One metaphor that's used to explain rebirth is that of two candles. Say I have a lit candle and use its flame to light a second candle. Then, let's say I blow out the first candle. Is the flame of the second candle the same as the first candle, or is it different? What would you say?

People often quickly assume that one of these statements is correct, that it's either the same flame or a different one. But we could actually make a case for both—or against both, for that matter. Is it the same flame? Well, yes, sort of. It's the continuation of the first flame, so we could say, in that broad sense, that it's the same flame. Is it a different flame? Well, again, yes, in a way. The flame of the second candle results from different bits of wax and wick, and from the combustion of different oxygen molecules than those of the first flame. With the incisive sword of Buddhist logic, we could, in fact, support any of the following four statements with some justification: it's the same flame as before, it's a different flame, it's both the same and different, or it's neither the same nor a different flame.

So what happens when we die? If the flame of our life energy crosses over to another life, are we the same person?

You Are Life Itself

First, let's revisit the flame of that first candle, all by itself. It seems to be a certain kind of thing, a "self," so to speak, something we recognize and call a candle flame. But the truth is more mysterious. The burning candle is actually a process of change and transformation. In every moment, new wax molecules are being burned. In every moment, new oxygen is being used. In every moment, the flame dies and is reborn.

If we grasp this fully—something that requires time and contemplation—we begin to see that death and life are interconnected all the time. The lurking monster turns out to be your familiar house cat. But to get there, your perspective needs to change. If you're still thinking of yourself as Harry Smith or Jane Doe, and if you identify with that person as a solid, concrete, and unchanging entity, you'll be full of fear. The monster will continue to terrify you. But insofar as you can see that you're a life process, a process without beginning or end, and identify with *that*, you've left fear behind. It depends completely on what you identify with.

When we let go of the idea of being a separate thing, an isolated self, when we stop identifying with such a viewpoint, our fear and struggle come to an end. We know ourselves as endless, unlimited life, inseparable from the rest of the universe, mysterious and unnamable. The elements that have come together to create us will come apart again and rejoin in countless other forms and patterns. Perhaps you could say you will "come back" as another person after you die. But you could also say that tomorrow you will be a flower, a cloud, or a tree standing in the wind on a mountaintop, enjoying yourself and unafraid.

Further, even now you are taking many other forms. Everyone whose life you have touched in some way—from giving them anything from a kind smile to lifesaving assistance—is also you, and you are also those people. Your life is in their lives, and their lives in yours. You inter-are. When you give money to feed children in a far-off place, you are reborn in them. As a therapist, I am reborn in those I've helped, not only in them but also in everyone connected to them. As an author and teacher, I likewise take many other forms. And so do you.

Similarly, if the Buddha has touched you, you are now a continuation of the Buddha. The Buddha lives in you. If the life and teaching of Christ have touched you, you are the continuation of Christ. If you've been touched deeply enough, you can even say, as Saint Paul does, "I, no longer I, but Christ in me" (Gal. 3:20; my translation). If a Buddhist teacher, a rabbi, a priest, or a minister has affected your life in a positive way, or if anyone has helped you through a difficult time by showing concern and love, you are the continuation of that person. You and that person inter-are.

We're like raindrops about to fall from a cloud. Maybe the raindrop will become a human being. Maybe it will flow into a river or rest in the ocean's depths. Whatever it becomes is just a matter of ongoing transformation—only the raindrop doesn't complain about it.

Reality Is Not Captured in Concepts

We might start off with a simple notion about death. Maybe we are materialists, and think of death as simply the end. Or maybe we are religious, and think of death as going to heaven. Maybe we think of it in terms of reincarnation and believe that we come back as another human being. But if we look more closely, we can see that all of these notions are too simplistic. We see that nothing is really born, and nothing really dies. Before I was born, I was already alive in my parents and ancestors, and in many other forms. After I die, I continue in many forms as well. Heaven is being fully alive in the here and now, not a place we go to after death. We see that reincarnation, taken literally, is also a little too simplistic, since we are dying and being reborn continually. We are this reality of wondrous becoming, a reality so mysterious that Buddhists call it *śūnyatā*, or emptiness (since to call it fullness would imply a limit to what is limitless).

In Buddhist terms, when we contemplate death and rebirth, we learn to avoid getting trapped in extreme views. Nature itself teaches that matter and energy are never destroyed, only transformed. Likewise, death is really a transformation. We go beyond the literal view. It's an ending but not just an ending. We see that reality is not so simple as being (*bhava*) or nonbeing (*abhava*). It's not so simple as permanence (*sassata*) or annihilation (*uccheda*). But it's something in between. What it is exactly, we can't say in words, any more than we could describe what coffee tastes like to someone who has never tasted it. To know, we must step beyond our concepts and experience it for ourselves.

To the extent, then, that we identify with the illusion of being a separate self, we suffer as death approaches. And to the extent that we identify with life itself, we are free from suffering, both now and at the time of our death.

Anathapindika was a merchant who, for many years, had been a devoted supporter of the Buddha and his community. When he was dying, he had great pain. The Buddha sent two of his advanced disciples to help him, Shariputra and Ananda. They taught him a series of meditation exercises to relieve his pain. These exercises involved a thoroughgoing disidentification with the physical self and brought Anathapindika great relief. He was then able to die peacefully and without fear.

Hearing about no self, great masters' deaths, or accounts of reincarnation may pique our interest, but they're not enough to bring us the gift of no fear. To receive that gift, we need our own insight. This exercise is a variation of the one that helped Anathapindika. If we are wise, we won't wait until we're dying to practice this.

Practice:
"I Am Life"

Do this exercise when you're not rushed and can take your time with each element.

Step 1: Take refuge. It's important to feel safe while doing an exercise like this. For this reason, the place to start is with taking refuge, as described in the prior chapter. When you have a sense of calm and safety, you are ready for the next step.

Step 2: This body is not me. Sit in meditation posture and settle into awareness of your breathing. Feel the calming pleasantness of breathing in and breathing out.

Bring up a sense of your body as whole. Breathe in and out with this sense of your whole body for several minutes.

Now practice with individual areas of the body. Tell yourself, "Breathing in, I am aware of my feet. Breathing out, I smile to my feet." After making more vivid contact with your feet, practice, "Breathing in and out, I know my feet are not me. I am more than my feet."

Then turn to your calves and practice the same way: "Breathing in, I'm aware of my calves. Breathing out, I smile to them." And then practice, "Breathing in and out, I know that my calves are not me. I am more than my calves."

Then, in turn, work with other areas of your body in the same way: your hands, forearms, upper arms, back, neck and shoulders, head and face, chest and abdomen, heart, lungs, and digestive organs.

Return to a sense of your body as a whole, and breathe in and out restfully with it.

Step 3: The senses are not me. Now begin to disidentify with your senses. In Buddhism, you may recall that there are six: sight, hearing, smell, taste, the feeling body, and the thinking mind.

Breathing in and out, become aware of your eyes. If you like, gently touch your closed eyelids with your hands to make contact with them in a concrete way. Practice like this: "Breathing in and out, I know my eyes are not me."

In the same way, practice with your ears, your nose, your tongue, the feeling body, and the thinking mind.

Step 4: The aggregates are not me. In the same way now, work with the five aggregates of form, feeling, perception, mental formation, and consciousness. Here "form" is the same as "body" in the previous step, so there's some overlap. This is okay. The idea is to have a rather thoroughgoing process of disidentification. Say, "This body is not me," "My feelings are not me," and so on.

Step 5: The elements are not me. In the ancient world, the universe was thought to be composed of earth, air, fire, and water. This way of describing things is still useful in meditation. The element earth is whatever is solid in us. Breathe in and out, knowing, "The element earth is not me." In the same way, contemplate, "The element air [the breath] is not me. The element fire [the heat in the body, the process of digestion, which generates heat] is not me. The element water [bodily fluids] is not me." Recognize that these four elements are also in everything else around you.

Step 6: I am life. Breathe in and out, dwelling quietly and unhurriedly with each of these statements in turn, opening to the reality they point to:

- I am not limited by this body, the six senses, the five aggregates, or the four elements.

- I am life itself.

- I am one life, undivided across space and time.

- I am life in all living beings on the earth now.

- I am life in all living beings in the future and in the past.

- I have never been born; I will never die.

Afterword

The first morning of September dawns cool and clear. As I practice walking meditation in the foothills of the Sandia mountains, I intentionally relax into the present moment. I am greeted not only by neighbors, but also by the wildflowers that blossom purple, yellow, and white. I feel a deep connection with the flowers, the rocks and trees, the hills, the birds, and the sky. And while my life, like yours, dear friend, has its share of difficulties, I confirm the central idea of this book: it is possible to find happiness by simply opening into the present moment, appreciating everything around us.

Happiness is the direct path. We don't need to establish anything else to be happy. We can be happy simply and directly by just learning to be present to the wonders around us.

When we are happy, we also enlarge our capacity to be present to what is difficult, to heal our sorrow, and to transform our pain. We see ways through our difficulties that previously lay hidden. And we become someone whose presence is reliable and helpful to others.

Practicing happiness is the greatest gift we give to ourselves, and, at the same time, to other people.

May you be happy!

Recommended Reading

Armstrong, Karen. 2001. *Buddha*. New York: Viking Penguin.

Beck, Charlotte Joko. 1989. *Everyday Zen: Love and Work*. San Francisco: HarperSanFrancisco.

Bien, Thomas, and Beverly Bien. 2002. *Mindful Recovery: A Spiritual Path to Healing from Addiction*. New York: John Wiley and Sons.

———. 2003. *Finding the Center Within: The Healing Way of Mindfulness Meditation*. Hoboken, NJ: John Wiley and Sons.

Boorstein, Sylvia. 1997. *It's Easier Than You Think: The Buddhist Way to Happiness*. San Francisco: HarperSanFrancisco.

Chödrön, Pema. 2001. *Start Where You Are: A Guide to Compassionate Living*. Boston: Shambhala Publications.

Fredrickson, Barbara L. 2009. *Positivity: Groundbreaking Research Reveals How to Embrace the Hidden Strength of Positive Emotions, Overcome Negativity, and Thrive*. New York: Crown Publishers.

Goldstein, Joseph. 1993. *Insight Meditation: The Practice of Freedom*. Boston: Shambhala Publications.

H.H. the Dalai Lama and Howard C. Cutler. 1998. *The Art of Happiness: A Handbook for Living*. New York: Riverhead Books.

Huxley, Aldous. 1945. *The Perennial Philosophy*. New York: Harper and Row.

Kabat-Zinn, Jon. 1990. *Full Catastrophe Living: Using the Wisdom of Your Body and Mind to Face Stress, Pain, and Illness*. New York: Delta.

———. 1994. *Wherever You Go, There You Are: Mindfulness Meditation in Everyday Life*. New York: Hyperion.

Kornfield, Jack. 1994. *Buddha's Little Instruction Book*. New York: Bantam Books.

———. 2000. *After the Ecstasy, the Laundry: How the Heart Grows Wise on the Spiritual Path*. New York: Bantam Books.

Lama Surya Das. 1997. *Awakening the Buddha Within: Eight Steps to Enlightenment—Tibetan Wisdom for the Western World*. New York: Broadway Books.

———. 1999. *Awakening to the Sacred: Creating a Spiritual Life from Scratch*. New York: Broadway Books.

———. 2000. *Awakening the Buddhist Heart: Integrating Love, Meaning, and Connection into Every Part of Your Life*. New York: Broadway Books.

———. 2003. *Letting Go of the Person You Used to Be: Lessons on Change, Loss, and Spiritual Transformation*. New York: Broadway Books.

Merton, Thomas. 1968. *The Asian Journals of Thomas Merton*. New York: New Directions Books.

Rosenberg, Larry. 1998. *Breath by Breath: The Liberating Practice of Insight Meditation*. With David Guy. Boston: Shambhala Publications.

Thich Nhat Hanh. 1992. *Peace Is Every Step: The Path of Mindfulness in Everyday Life*. New York: Bantam Books.

———. 2007. *The Art of Power*. New York: HarperCollins.

Willliams, Mark, John Teasdale, Zindel Segal, and Jon Kabat-Zinn. 2007. *The Mindful Way Through Depression: Freeing Yourself from Chronic Unhappiness*. New York: The Guilford Press.

References

Barasch, Marc Ian. 2005. *Field Notes on the Compassionate Life: A Search for the Soul of Kindness.* New York: Rodale.

Bayda, Ezra. 2008. *Zen Heart: Simple Advice for Living with Mindfulness and Compassion.* Boston: Shambhala Publications.

Becker, Ernest. 1973. *The Denial of Death.* New York: The Free Press.

Blackman, Sushila, ed. 2005. *Graceful Exits: How Great Beings Die—Death Stories of Tibetan, Hindu, and Zen Masters.* Boston: Shambhala Publications.

Buxbaum, Yitzhak. 2004. *The Life and Teachings of Hillel.* Lanham, MD: Rowman and Littlefield Publishers.

Forstater, Mark. 2000. *The Spiritual Teachings of Marcus Aurelius.* New York: HarperCollins.

Hanson, Rick. 2009. *Buddha's Brain: The Practical Neuroscience of Happiness, Love, and Wisdom.* With Richard Mendius. Oakland, CA: New Harbinger Publications.

Kessler, David A. 2009. *The End of Overeating: Taking Control of the Insatiable American Appetite.* New York: Rodale.

Kornfield, Jack. 1996. *Living Dharma: Teachings of Twelve Buddhist Masters.* Boston: Shambhala Publications.

Longfellow, H. W. 2001. *Poems and Other Writings.* New York: Library of America.

Maslow, Abraham H. 1968. *Toward a Psychology of Being.* 2nd ed. Princeton: Van Nostrand Reinhold.

McClelland, David C. 1986. Some reflections on the two psychologies of love. *Journal of Personality* 54(2):344–49.

McKay, Matthew, Peter D. Rogers, and Judith McKay. 1989. *When Anger Hurts: Quieting the Storm Within.* Oakland, CA: New Harbinger Publications.

Mitchell, Stephen. 1991. *The Gospel According to Jesus: A New Translation and Guide to His Essential Teachings for Believers and Unbelievers.* New York: HarperCollins.

Rahula, Walpola. 1974. *What the Buddha Taught.* 2nd ed. New York: Grove Press.

Rogers, Carl R. 1957. The necessary and sufficient conditions of therapeutic personality change. *Journal of Consulting Psychology* 21(2):95–103.

Seligman, Martin E. P. 1998. *Learned Optimism: How to Change Your Mind and Your Life.* New York: Pocket Books.

Stevenson, Ian. 1974. *Twenty Cases Suggestive of Reincarnation.* 2nd ed. Charlottesville, VA: University Press of Virginia.

Thich Nhat Hanh. 1988. *The Heart of Understanding: Commentaries on the Prajñaparamita Heart Sutra.* Berkeley, CA: Parallax Press.

———. 1990. *Transformation and Healing: Sutra on the Four Establishments of Mindfulness.* Berkeley, CA: Parallax Press.

———. 1993. *Thundering Silence: Sutra on Knowing the Better Way to Catch a Snake.* Berkeley, CA: Parallax Press.

———. 1996. *Breathe! You Are Alive: Sutra on the Full Awareness of Breathing.* Berkeley, CA: Parallax Press.

———. 1998. *The Heart of the Buddha's Teaching: Transforming Suffering into Peace, Joy, and Liberation.* Berkeley, CA: Parallax Press.

———. 2002. *Be Free Where You Are.* Berkeley, CA: Parallax Press.

———. 2009. *You Are Here: Discovering the Magic of the Present Moment.* Boston: Shambhala Publications.

Watts, Alan W. 1957. *The Way of Zen.* New York: Vintage Books.

Weiss, Brian L. 1988. *Many Lives, Many Masters: The True Story of a Prominent Psychiatrist, His Young Patient, and the Past-Life Therapy That Changed Both Their Lives.* New York: Simon and Schuster.

Yongey Mingyur Rinpoche. 2007. *The Joy of Living: Unlocking the Secret and Science of Happiness.* With Eric Swanson. New York: Three Rivers Press.

Thomas Bien, Ph.D., is a psychologist in private practice in Albuquerque, NM, where he also teaches mindfulness and meditation. He is author of numerous scientific articles and book chapters in psychology, especially in the areas of spirituality and addiction. He is author of *Mindful Recovery*, *Finding the Center Within*, and *Mindful Therapy*. With Steven F. Hick, Ph.D., he is coeditor of *Mindfulness and the Therapeutic Relationship*.

Foreword writer **Lama Surya Das** is a lineage holder in the Dzogchen tradition of Tibetan Buddhism residing in Cambridge, MA. He is founder of Dzogchen Center and author of many books. The Dalai Lama calls him "The American Lama."